RELIGIOUS STUDIES COURSE

Christian Perspectives on Contemporary Issues

by
DIANA MORGAN

(Also author of 'Jesus in the Synoptic Gospels')

GW00359461

CONTENTS

THE CANTERBURY PRESS NORWICH

PREFACE FOR TEACHERS

This course is designed to meet the needs of GCSE but also provides many activities and discussion topics suitable for General Studies or modules of PSE (Personal and Social Education) courses.

The book is suitable for use with the syllabuses of the principal examining boards. National criteria require GCSE candidates' ability to be assessed in the following areas:

1. Selection and presentation of factual information.
2. Understanding of a variety of religious concepts and responses.
3. Evaluation of issues of belief and practice.

Therefore the questions provided in each unit cover these three areas. Each unit ends with suggestions for coursework.

Every unit follows the same basic pattern:

1. Questions to stimulate thought or discussion.
2. Factual information on which informed opinion can be based.
3. Christian perspectives on the particular issue.

The GCSE teachers' guide for religious studies states 'students should be primarily aware that religion is a living experience and they should have the opportunity to explore it through the practices, values and attitudes of believers today'. Christian practices, values and attitudes are therefore explained when appropriate. It is for the teacher to ensure that students are not inhibited from questioning the views expressed. In this way they can be helped to understand what is meant by a religious view of life and begin to try to make sense of human experience for themselves. The units may, if you prefer, be studied in any order.

Cross-references are supplied if information relevant to a particular unit has been covered earlier in the book. In this way it is possible for teachers to forge cross-curricular links so that students bring interests aroused in other areas of their study to religious issues.

'... not inhibited from questioning the views expressed.'

First published 1990 by The Canterbury Press Norwich,
(an imprint of Hymns Ancient & Modern Ltd),
St Mary's Works, St Mary's Plain, Norwich, Norfolk, NR3 3BH

British Library Cataloguing in Publication Data
Morgan, Diana, 1931–
    Christian perspectives on contemporary issues.
    1. Society—Christian viewpoints
    I. Title   II. Series
    261

ISBN 1-85311-010-8

Typeset by Eta Services (Typesetters) Ltd, Beccles, Suffolk.
Printed and bound in Great Britain by St Edmundsbury Press, Suffolk

TO START YOU TALKING

1. Work in pairs

Think of someone in the room whom you like and, without naming him/her, describe that person until your partner recognises him/her. What is it which makes it possible to identify the individual? Is it physical features? mannerisms? personality? something else?

2. Work on your own

Now consider a friend.

(a) What is it about him/her you particularly like? Sense of humour? Brains? Kindness? Good looks? It is difficult to pinpoint qualities, but do the best you can. Is this the whole truth about your friend?

(b) Imagine an X-ray picture of your friend. Does this give a true picture? But is it the whole truth?
(c) Imagine an oil painting of the same person. In what ways does this view differ from a snapshot? Which is true?
(d) Now try to see that same friend through your teacher's eyes. What differences appear?
(e) Imagine the same person at home with his or her family. Does this give you yet another side of the truth?

It is not possible to say that any one of these views contains the whole truth making the other views false. All are different versions of the same person.

If you can absorb and hold in your mind more than one view of a person, there is no reason why you should not similarly be able to hold in balance scientific, sociological and religious views of life, recognising each as true but in different ways. It is important that you should try to do this throughout this course.

INFORMATION

William Barclay quotes an American chemical analysis of man. The average individual contains:

> Enough fat to make seven bars of soap
> Enough iron to make a medium sized nail
> Enough sugar to fill a sugar sifter
> Enough lime to whitewash a henhouse
> Enough potassium to explode a toy cannon
> Enough magnesium for a dose of magnesia
> Enough phosphorous to make tips for two thousand two hundred matches

Add a very little sulphur and five buckets of water and you have all the materials needed to make a man. *What is missing?*

Further fascinating facts might be added. It seems each of us contains about sixty thousand *miles* of blood vessels and that, if it were possible to spread out the air sacs of one person's lungs, they would cover a tennis court.

Surely this is enough to make us marvel and yet . . . is that *all* we are? Of course not. We are all changed and shaped by the relationships we experience in society and have a spiritual side which develops (or fails to develop) through our relationship with God.

CHRISTIAN PERSPECTIVES

Christians, in common with religious people of many other faiths, believe that God created the universe and all it contains and that human beings are able to co-operate with God.

> **SUGGESTIONS FOR BIBLE STUDY**
> **Genesis 1–3**

1. CREATION STORIES

There are two separate accounts of creation in the book of Genesis. They can be understood in different ways i.e.

(a) As history and science. Some people believe that God actually created the world in the way Genesis describes; that two people called Adam and Eve really did say and do more or less what Genesis says they did. Those who hold this belief are called **fundamentalists**.
(b) As stories written to describe human nature and the will of God. Stories of this kind are sometimes called **myths**. They do not have to be historically or scientifically true any more than the words of pop songs have to be true-as-science in order to be true about human nature.

When Christians read stories which were written two or three thousand years ago they do not expect to find direct answers to modern problems but they believe that the Bible provides pointers to the way God

3

intends his world to run and that it tells us much about human beings and their relationship to God and to one another.

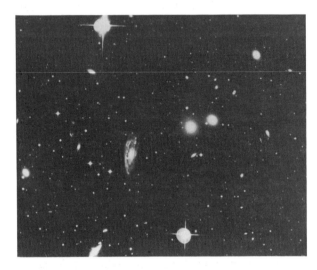

Read the first Creation story, (Gen. 1.1–2.4) and then give verse numbers to match the following statements:

(a) The world was created by God.
(b) People were created in God's image (i.e. basically good).
(c) They were given authority over the rest of creation to rule it on God's behalf.
(d) Sexuality is God-given and therefore good in itself.
(e) The need for a balance between work and rest is built into Creation.

2. STORY OF THE FALL

Read the story in Genesis 3 observing that Adam and Eve behave just as we do.

Now take each of the following points in the story and apply them to modern life:

(a) Temptation is subtle, appealing to pride (Gen. 3.5)
Give examples from your own experience of temptations which appeal to pride.
(b) Having done wrong, Eve wants someone to share her wrong-doing and tempts the person closest to her (Gen. 3.6)
Check in any newspaper how many of the cases brought before a court involve more than one defendant.
(c) When they realise they are not as clever as they thought (Gen. 3.7), Adam and Eve try to hide themselves.
How do we ourselves try to hide wrongdoing in ordinary daily life? Think of a variety of ways (our 'fig-leaves'!).
(d) God does not leave them alone in their sin. He visits them (Gen. 3.8–9).
How does God 'visit' people today?
(e) They cannot face him and blame everyone but themselves.
Count how many times in a day you say/hear someone else say 'It wasn't me.'!
(f) Yet God still takes care of Adam and Eve (Gen. 3.21).
Suggest ways in which God's care for people is shown in the modern world.

UNIT 2   Ethics

When we speak of ethics we mean a set of principles which guide behaviour. Sometimes the difference between right and wrong is obvious but in many situations it is difficult to decide what is right and people reach different conclusions in good faith.

TO START YOU TALKING

1. *Work in pairs*

Which of these decisions involves a moral choice?
(a) Whether to visit a friend in hospital or go to the pub.
(b) Whether to go to a football match or play snooker.
(c) Whether to lend a friend your homework to copy.

(d) Whether to tell a friend his/her new and expensive hairstyle is a big mistake.
(e) Whether to travel half-fare on the bus.
(f) Whether to sleep with your girl/boyfriend.
(g) Whether to take a Saturday job.
(h) Whether to risk driving when you suspect you may be very slightly drunk.
(i) Whether to take part in strike action.
(j) Whether to stand for the local council.

2. *Work in fours*

A Balloon Debate
Four people are in a hot-air balloon which is unaccountably losing height. If they are not all to perish the best hope is to lighten the load by throwing out passengers. In which order would you throw them out? They are:

(i) A scientist who has discovered a cure for AIDS but has not yet had time to make it public.
(ii) An elderly engineer who might yet succeed in saving the balloon.
(iii) The mother of a young baby.
(iv) Mother Teresa.

INFORMATION

There are two main ways of dealing with moral choices:

1. MORAL ABSOLUTES

This involves having a set of rules in which some things are right (good), others are wrong (bad). An example of a set of rules is the ten commandments. These are sometimes referred to as the decalogue (Greek *dekalogos* = ten words). You will find them in full in Exodus 20.1–17 but they can be summarised as follows:

> I am the Lord your God.
> You must have no other gods before me.
> You must not blaspheme.
> Keep the Sabbath day holy.
> Honour your father and mother.
> You must not murder.
> You must not commit adultery.
> You must not steal.
> You must not lie.
> You must not covet (*What does 'covet' mean?*)

You need to learn the ten commandments by heart.

Notice that they divide into two 'tables of the law' – duty to God and duty to others. *How many commandments are in each?* Rules seek to enforce a way of life which benefits society and to discourage actions which harm people. On the other hand, they can be rigid to the point where 'the law is an ass'.

Is it possible to 'get round' the ten commandments without actually breaking them?

TEST YOURSELF ON FACTS
1. What is meant by ethics?
2. Name two commandments about duty to God.
3. Name three commandments about duty to others.
4. (a) What are the things the last commandment forbids our coveting? (You will have to look up Ex. 20.)
   (b) Think of twentieth century equivalents.
5. What is meant by 'moral absolutes'?
6. What is meant by 'situation ethics'?

2. SITUATION ETHICS

Some people believe that there are no moral absolutes, i.e. goodness and badness can be different in different situations. That is what is meant by situation ethics. For example, the commandment 'You shall not steal' is a moral absolute. Stealing is wrong and forbidden. But suppose a mother were to steal in order to feed her starving child. In that situation is stealing wrong? Situation ethics is a way of looking at life which we shall have to take into account in considering many of the moral issues on which decisions have to be made. In situation ethics the only thing which is always unfailingly good is love. So, in every situation, a person has to work out what love requires rather than acting according to rules.

WHAT DO YOU THINK?

Did the mother do right in the following well-known story?
A party of settlers travelling west across America were hiding from Indians. A baby belonging to a mother in the group started to cry and the mother promptly strangled her child to save the party from discovery.

3. MORALITY AND LAW

It is also necessary to distinguish between what is immoral and what is illegal. For example, homosexual practices used to be illegal but nowadays, within certain limits, this is no longer so. Not everyone would agree that homosexual practices are morally acceptable so, because an action is *legal* it does not necessarily mean it is *moral*.

CHECK YOUR UNDERSTANDING

Rule up four columns on the right-hand side of a page in your books and head them: Legal, Moral, Illegal, Immoral. Copy out the following situations down the left-hand side and then tick the appropriate columns in each case.
(a) *Travelling half-fare on the bus when you are 16.*
(b) *Buying alcoholic drink in a supermarket when you are 16.*
(c) *Crossing against the lights at a pelican crossing.*
(d) *Not pointing out a mistake in change to a shopkeeper.*
(e) *Lying to get out of trouble.*

If you have time, think up some more situations for yourself.

CHRISTIAN PERSPECTIVES

SUGGESTIONS FOR BIBLE STUDY
Ex. 20.1–17   Luke 15.11–32
Matt. 5.21–48   Romans 13.8–10

Christians try to live according to the ten commandments but Jesus went further in his teaching. He believed that people should look to their inner motives. His teaching is summarised in part of the Sermon on the Mount (Matt. 5.21–48) where he gives the commandments an inward interpretation which makes them much more difficult to keep.

Read the passage for yourself. What does Jesus say is as serious as murder? What does he say is as serious as adultery? How are Christians told to behave towards those who ill-use them?

The Sermon on the Mount sets an impossible standard ('Be ye perfect') and reveals the paradox (= apparent absurd contradiction) at the heart of the Christian attitude to life. Nobody can be perfect but when Christians fail they are taught to turn back to God and to ask forgiveness. In this way (i.e. drawing closer to God when they are sorry) Christians believe that very, very gradually they will be changed. *Through* failure, therefore, a person can grow spiritually.

COURSEWORK

Study the parable of the prodigal son (Luke 15.11–32). It is a parable which illustrates Jesus' teaching about forgiveness. Think carefully about each of the characters in turn. If you are stuck you will find a few ideas in Unit 6 p. 18. Then choose a parallel modern situation and write a play on the same theme. If possible, perform it in Assembly.

UNIT 3   Love. Sexual Ethics

TO START YOU TALKING

Work in pairs

1. Here is a list of qualities you might hope to find in a friend. Arrange them in the order you think most important. Consider them first in relation to someone of

your own sex and secondly in relation to someone of the opposite sex.

> Similarity of interest: loyalty: mutual respect: kindness: good looks: generosity: an interest in you yourself as a person: honesty: tolerance: similarity of age.

2. Make a list of the songs in the charts at the present time which are about love. How many are there? What do they tell us about the experience?

3. Your sister confides in you that her boyfriend has suggested that they should sleep together to make sure they really are suited to each other. What advice would you give? Would the advice differ if you were (a) her parents, (b) a priest, (c) a doctor, (d) a solicitor?

INFORMATION

1. DIFFERENT KINDS OF LOVE

The Greeks had four different words for love which distinguish between different kinds of love. They are:

(a) *Storgé*   (say *store-gay*)
   This is having a warm regard for something ('I love school/football/that dress'). There is no sexual ele-

ment in it and, although we should not like to lose the object of our affection, we are not unduly upset if that should happen.

(b) *Philia*   (say *filly-ar*)
   This is best translated as friendship. It occurs between equals and describes the relationship between friends. We do not share the whole of our lives with friends but have a sense of loyalty to them and it hurts if the relationship ends.

(c) *Eros*   (say *ear-ross*)
   This is the state of 'falling in love'. It is based on emotions and the physical attraction of one sex for the other. In this state it is difficult to think straight. We see the other person through rose-tinted spectacles and, even if we are aware that we are doing so, we seem unable to help ourselves.

(d) *Agapé*   (say *agga-pea*)
   This is the word used by St Paul in a famous passage describing Christian love (1 Corinth. 13). It is the kind of love which always puts the other person first, however much it may hurt to do so and even if that love is not returned. It does not depend on emotions but involves accepting other people as they are. In this sense it is possible to say 'I do not really *like* you but I *love* you'.

Copy out the following situations in your books. Make up your minds which kind of love each involves and write the appropriate Greek word beside it. If you have time, think of more for yourselves.

> (i) The 'love' which develops between the members of a team.
>
> (ii) A 'love' of baked beans.
>
> (iii) The 'love' shown by a mother for her child.
>
> (iv) The 'love' which sets you tingling at the sight of him/her.
>
> (v) The 'love' which sends a lifeboat crew out in a storm.

We learn to give love through being loved ourselves, and we need to receive love as well as to give it. One cause of marriage breakdown is an inability to contribute to this two-way process. A person who has never received love will have great difficulty in giving it.

2. SEXUAL ETHICS

Is it wrong to have sexual intercourse outside marriage?

(A) Sexuality and the law

(a) 'Age of consent'

It is illegal in this country for a man to have sexual intercourse with a girl under the age of 16. This is the age when the girl is supposed to understand what she is doing. There are many who would like to see the age of consent lowered on the grounds that girls mature earlier than they did in the days when the law was passed. Before making up your own mind, read about the work of Josephine Butler who was one of many who strove hard to have the age *raised* to 16 (p. 10).

(b) *Homosexuality*

In 1957 the Wolfenden Committee on Homosexual Offences and Prostitution recommended that homo-

TEST YOURSELF ON FACTS

1. What is the Greek word which describes Christian love?
2. What is the age of consent? What does the term mean?
3. What subject did the Wolfenden Committee investigate?
4. What is the main provision of the 1967 Sex Offences Act?
5. Read 1 Corinth. 13 and then make a list of ten qualities of love described in the text.

sexual acts between consenting adults (i.e. 21 years and over) in private should no longer be a criminal offence. The Report said that some areas of private morality were not the law's business. These recommendations were incorporated into the 1967 Sex Offences Act.

(B) Sex Outside Marriage

Do you think it makes any difference morally if a couple are co-habiting (= living together) on a more or less permanent basis without marrying? What reasons can you suggest for living together without marrying? Would the arrival of a baby change your opinion? Give reasons.

In the past, two practical considerations helped to uphold traditional teaching that a sexual relationship should be confined to marriage – fear of pregnancy and fear of disease. These factors still need to be taken into account.

(a) *Fear of pregnancy*

Statistics suggest that, even though some forms of contraception are readily available, there are many who, for one reason or another, do not use them. For example, the number of conceptions which led to abortion was as follows:

Age of woman	1971	1988
Under 16	2,000	4,000
Age 16–19	19,000	41,000
Age 20–34	60,000	116,000

In 1961 six per cent of live births were illegitimate. By 1988 that percentage had risen to twenty-five.

CHECK YOUR UNDERSTANDING

1. Look at the statistics of the number of conceptions which led to abortion. Draw a graph to express the figures. Can you suggest reasons for the enormous increase?
2. Having read 1 Corinth. 13, explain the meaning of the passage from 'Love will never come to an end . . . but the greatest of them all is love'.

(b) *Fear of disease*

Until recently modern drugs had reduced fear of sexually transmitted diseases but AIDS is changing attitudes. Of all sexually transmitted diseases it is the one for which at present there is no cure, and death is practically certain. One thing must be made clear. It would be quite wrong to say that a particular disease is God's punishment for a particular form of wrongdoing. Suffering is a mystery. We do not understand why some good people suffer and some evil ones prosper. On the other hand, certain actions are known to have certain consequences. If I insist on driving when I am drunk, I cannot say God is punishing me if I am involved in an accident. Similarly we can say that in some cases the spread of AIDS is the result of ignoring sexual restraints. Furthermore innocent people are caught up in the consequences as in the case of drunken driving.

WHAT DO YOU THINK?
1. Is it possible to make laws about morality? What are the pitfalls?
2. Can you suggest what the Christian attitude might be towards someone suffering from AIDS?

(C) Homosexuality

No accurate statistics are available of the number of homosexuals in Britain. We do not know what causes this state. It needs to be said that many teenagers are happier with members of their own sex. This does not mean that they will not develop into heterosexual adults. Experts know that some people do not settle into a permanent sexual orientation until their mid-twenties.

CHRISTIAN PERSPECTIVES

SUGGESTIONS FOR BIBLE STUDY
Gen. 1. 27–28: 2.18   Matt. 5.27–30
1 Corinth. 6.19–20; 13

---

1. Agapé

The best-known description of Christian love (agapé) is contained in St Paul's first letter to the Corinthians, which you should read for yourselves and then answer the questions on it contained in the boxes in this Unit.

2. Relationships between the sexes

Love is at the heart of the Christian understanding of the relationship between the sexes and love brings responsibility for the person loved. Sexual intercourse is seen by Christians as the highest form of love-making when people make a total commitment to each other. For this reason in the New Testament alone sexual intercourse between unmarried people is condemned at least eighteen times.

What is lacking if it is used only as a means of self-gratification?

3. Homosexuality

A distinction has to be made between what is legal and what is moral. The Bible condemns homosexuality as sin but the Church in its teaching makes a difference between homosexual relationships and homosexual acts. Love comes from God and there is nothing wrong in *love* between people of the same sex, but the expression of that love in homosexual *acts* is condemned by most Christians as sin. For Roman Catholics such acts are forbidden because they cannot lead to new life. Some of the churches take a more liberal view. A Report from the Church of England expresses understanding for homosexuals who 'through no fault of their own, find themselves in a situation of great difficulty in which many of the moral guidelines normally available do not apply and in which there is little general sympathy or understanding'. (*Homosexual Relationships published by the Board for Social Responsibility*), and warns against people making sweeping condemnations when they cannot know all the circumstances.

4. A Matching Game

Here are some biblical insights into sexuality. Match the statements to the Bible references given in the Box. Do you agree or disagree with them?

(a) Sexuality is God-given and good in itself.
(b) Sexuality is the way in which human beings co-operate with God in creation.
(c) Our need for relationships is God-given and is not to be used selfishly.
(d) God has a claim on the use we make of the body he has given us.
(e) Adultery has been committed as soon as the wish to do so has been allowed to take root.

COURSEWORK
Make a survey of attitudes towards sex outside marriage in order to find out the differences between your own, your parents' and your grandparents' generation. Is a different attitude towards virginity expected of men and women? Try to assess the reasons for the attitudes you find. What part is played by (i) fear, (ii) faith? Then write a report on your findings.

Josephine Butler

(1828–1906)

What could have made a clever, charming woman from a comfortable middle-class background living in Victorian England take up the cause of young prostitutes and give them shelter in her own home?

To help you imagine the situation you need to know that in those days women were subject to the Contagious Diseases Acts. Had you been a woman living in any of the garrison or dockyard towns such as Aldershot or Chatham and somebody named you as a prostitute you could have been forced to undergo a medical examination to make sure you were not suffering from disease which might infect your supposed customers. There was no need for evidence; that would have embarrassed the men involved. If you refused to have the examination you were thrown into prison. Whatever the verdict your reputation was likely to be ruined.

Josephine Butler saw that women were being degraded so that the health of men using prostitutes could be protected by law and fought against these discriminatory laws for twenty years. She addressed meetings all over this country and in Europe. Remember that women did not have the vote and her campaigning had to be carried on before audiences of men. She was shouted down, ridiculed, even attacked and yet she persevered in her determination to uphold the human

dignity of women who were powerless to help themselves. 'I am not here to represent virtuous women', she was to say on one occasion. 'I plead for the rights of the most virtuous and the most vicious equally.' It was not until 1883 that the Contagious Diseases Acts were suspended, being finally repealed in 1886.

Josephine Butler had been born in Northumberland in 1828 and died there in 1906. She received a good education and was sufficiently fluent in French and Italian to be able to address mass meetings as effectively in these languages as in English. At the age of 24 she married George Butler, a brilliant academic. After their marriage he was ordained and became in due course a headmaster and eventually a canon of Winchester cathedral. Josephine Butler had always been a campaigner but in 1864 their young daughter died in a terrible accident at their home in Cheltenham. The couple moved to Liverpool two years later and, looking beyond the home for activities to ease her grief, she soon saw that unemployment and poverty drove many women to prostitution. In 1869 she wrote, 'Among the 9000 women who are pursuing this calling in one of our great seaports, a late inquiry showed that 1500 were under 15 years of age and of these a third were under 13 years of age.' The age of consent was 12.

Josephine Butler campaigned to have that age of consent raised so that girls could be protected by law. Eventually she succeeded when the Criminal Law Amendment Act of 1885 raised the age of consent to 16.

Concern for prostitutes as human beings was not the only campaign fought by Josephine Butler. She realised that unemployment drove many of them on to the streets and believed that, given the opportunity of education, they would stand a better chance of finding work. 'Economics lie at the very root of practical morality,' she was to say. Just as important was the need for the vote. She knew from bitter experience in her own campaigns what an uphill struggle it would be to have the needs of women taken seriously. But she persevered. Josephine Butler's work was an expression of her Christian faith.

● *Look again carefully at the Christian Perspectives you have studied in the first three units of this book. Which ones can you identify in the life and work of Josephine Butler?*

TO START YOU TALKING

What rights do you think all the people involved in an abortion have? The people concerned are:

The mother: the father: families – grandparents, any other children: the foetus: the medical staff involved.

INFORMATION

1. ABORTION

(A) The Law

As you read this section find the answers to the first two questions in the 'Test Yourself on Facts' box.

Two laws are applicable to the rights of the unborn child:

(a) *1929 The Infant Life Preservation Act*
This act makes it illegal to destroy the life of a child *capable of being born alive* and sets the period of pregnancy after which this is possible at 28 weeks.

(b) *1967 Abortion Act*
This Act allows a pregnancy to be ended on any of the following grounds:

  (i) Risk to the life of the mother.
  (ii) Risk of injury to her physical or mental health.
  (iii) A substantial risk that, if the child were born, it would suffer from physical or mental abnormal-

ities. Nobody may be forced to take part in an abortion, except in cases where there is a risk to life. (This clause was designed to protect the rights of any doctors and nurses who believe abortion to be wrong. There is suspicion that it has had the effect of restricting the career prospects of such people.) The decision about whether there should be an abortion is to be taken by two doctors.

(c) *David Alton Bill*
In 1988 the Democrat MP David Alton introduced a Bill into parliament designed to reduce the period during which a woman may have an abortion to 18 weeks. As a Roman Catholic he made it clear that he himself was totally opposed to abortion and regarded 18 weeks as a compromise. It seemed likely that parliament would agree to a reduction from 28 weeks to at least 24 weeks but opponents of the Bill used delaying tactics so that it was killed for want of time.

(B) Statistics

The total number of abortions to women resident in Great Britain in 1988 was 180,000 an increase of almost 14 per cent on the previous year and of more than 50 per cent over the figure for 1971. In 1969 there were 50,000 abortions.

Why do you think there has been such a massive increase in the number of abortions since the legalising of abortion? Is the Act itself responsible for the number of unwanted pregnancies? Does the law influence moral attitudes?

David
Alton, M.P.

TEST YOURSELF ON FACTS

1. What are the main provisions of the 1967 Abortion Act?
2. What part has David Alton played in the debate over abortion?
3. What are the two extreme views on abortion?
4. In the opinion of the Church of England, what circumstances might justify abortion?
5. Who was Dr Leonard Arthur?

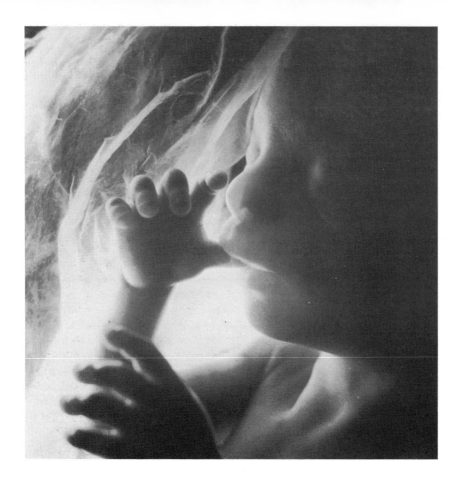

World famous photographer Lennart Nilsson took this remarkable picture of an 18 week baby in the womb sucking his thumb. © Lennart Nilsson

2. INFANTICIDE

Closely linked to the question of abortion is that of keeping alive babies born with various handicaps. The poet Clough wrote

'Thou shalt not kill; but need'st not strive
Officiously to keep alive.' (*What does 'officiously' mean?*)

In the twentieth century his words seem to have taken on a life of their own.

A Test Case

In 1981 a prosecution was brought against Dr Leonard Arthur, a paediatrician, on a charge of attempting to murder a new-born baby suffering from Down's Syndrome. (*Had you been the doctor, what would you have done in these circumstances?*) Any doctor in this situation has to juggle with three factors which vary, i.e.

(i) The medical condition of the child which can range from 'normal' to a completely cabbage-like state.
(ii) The attitude of the parents, which can vary between acceptance and total rejection.

(iii) A decision over treatment which can range from doing nothing to using the most up-to-date techniques.

In this particular case the parents had rejected the baby and so the doctor had ordered sufficient neglect in treatment to hasten death along the lines described in Clough's poem. Everyone from the judge downward paid tribute to the kindness and humanity of the doctor. The trial was really about what *any* doctor should do in these very difficult circumstances. Dr Arthur was acquitted but the debate went on.

WHAT DO YOU THINK?

Does Society have a duty to help doctors to make difficult ethical decisions, or do you think such decisions only concern those immediately involved in the problem?

CHRISTIAN PERSPECTIVES

SUGGESTIONS FOR BIBLE STUDY

Gen. 1.26–28   Mark 9.36–37
Gen. 4.9

CHECK YOUR UNDERSTANDING

Summarise what each of the suggested Bible passages is saying which is relevant to the debate on abortion/infanticide.

1. ABORTION

There are two extreme views:

(a) The life of the foetus must be preserved at all costs. The United Nations Declaration of Rights of the Child (1959) seems to support this view in declaring *'the child, by reason of his physical and mental immaturity, needs special safeguards and care, including appropriate legal protection, before as well as after birth'*.

(b) The mother has an absolute right to decide whether to bear the child she has conceived.

Christians themselves are divided over the issue.

(a) THE ROMAN CATHOLIC CHURCH is opposed to abortion in any circumstances, even rape or the certainty of giving birth to a severely handicapped child. Cardinal Basil Hume, Roman Catholic Archbishop of Westminster, has said, 'As a human being, there is surely a deep revulsion in most of us at the destruction of any human life in any form, including that in the womb ... If you really respect other people and really love other people, then the idea of taking life at any stage is inexplicable.'
Notice his emphasis on the two elements of respect for other people and love, which occur again and again in any discussion of Christian ethics.

(b) A less strict view is taken by another group called CHRISTIANS FOR FREE CHOICE which includes many members of the Free churches. They believe that the matter should be left to the individual woman's conscience. They recognise the difficulty of, for example, a pregnant teenager in making such a decision at a time when she is emotionally upset but firmly believe that such decisions should not be imposed by others.

(c) THE CHURCH OF ENGLAND, holding the middle ground, states that abortion is always an evil to be avoided if at all possible. However, it could be justified in three circumstances:
   (i) If there were a risk to the life of the mother or to her mental and physical health (*how is this to be defined?*).
   (ii) If she were likely to give birth to a deformed child.
   (iii) In the aftermath of rape.

2. INFANTICIDE

As in the case of abortion, the issue centres on the sanctity of human life and whether anyone has the right to assess either the value of the baby's life or the capacity of the parents to care for a handicapped child.

The Chief Rabbi, Sir Immanuel Jakobovits, made a statement on behalf of all Jews which puts in a nutshell the case for preserving life at all costs. He said that every human life is infinitely precious and that the views of the baby's parents and the views of the doctors are irrelevant. Any grading of human beings into those with a 'superior' and others with an 'inferior' claim to life is utterly repugnant to Judaism. The teaching of the Roman Catholic Church is similar. Other Christians put more emphasis on the capacity of the mother to cope. You have to make up your own minds on this very difficult issue, recognising that people of good faith will come to very different conclusions.

List the following attitudes to abortion in the order you think most important, putting any you strongly disagree with at the end:

> *'It's my body and I have the right to choose whether or not to bear the child I have conceived.'*
> *'It's murder.'*
> *'The foetus is not really a person.'*
> *'The child would be a baby for a childless couple to adopt.'*
> *'Abortion is just another form of birth control.'*
> *'As a child of God, I must use his power to produce life responsibly.'*
> *'The innocent and helpless must be protected at all costs.'*
> *'I would always feel guilty afterwards.'*

COURSEWORK

Write to organisations on both sides of the abortion debate for information about their points of view (addresses at the back of the book – don't forget to enclose a stamp). When you receive the information make a summary of both sides of the question and finish with a paragraph about your own views.

UNIT 5 — Marriage

TO START YOU TALKING

1. *On your own*

Decide the order of importance of the following qualities in a marriage partner:

- patience
- forgiveness
- being a good cook
- sense of humour
- faithfulness
- being sexually experienced
- being generous with money
- being prepared to share the chores
- sharing religious faith.

2. *In pairs*

Make a list of the things you think you need to know something about before you marry. Then discuss your lists with the rest of the class.

INFORMATION

1. LEGAL AND SOCIAL ASPECTS

A person has to be over 16 to marry and needs parental consent until the age of 18. Everyone has a right in law to be married in the parish church provided they live in the parish and as long as they have not been previously married.

These are practical matters. Society and the law are concerned with a person's status, i.e. we are all either single, married, widowed or divorced. This aspect of marriage is governed by law and does not require a 'church' wedding. In fact many couples prefer a Register Office ceremony. But all marriages need the support of society. Marriage is not a private matter but concerns the whole community.

Work out for yourselves why this should be so.

2. REQUIREMENTS IN MARRIAGE

There are three basic elements in marriage. (*You can remember them because they all begin with P*):

(a) **Permanence**
The Church of England marriage service still includes the words 'till death us do part'.

(b) **Personal loyalty**
The relationship is between one man and one woman. The Register Office ceremony includes the words 'Marriage according to the law of this country is the union of one man with one woman, voluntarily entered into for life to the exclusion of all others,' and the Anglican service says the same thing more poetically.

'Will you take *N* to be your wife (husband)? Will you love her (him), comfort her (him), honour and protect her (him) and forsaking all others, be faithful to her (him) as long as you both shall live?'

(c) **Possibility of procreation**
Although some couples will not have children, marriage is designed to provide the stable family life which children need.

In other words, the physical union through sexual intercourse is enfolded in a promise of being faithful to each other in a lifelong relationship. This state of having only one marriage partner is known as **monogamy**. (**Polygamy** = having more than one partner.) Because marriage is so important, both to the individuals and to the community, all societies make it the occasion of public ceremonial in which family and friends share the joy of bride and groom.

3. STATISTICS

In 1988 there were 394,000 marriages in the United Kingdom, 50 per cent of them in a Register Office. Of those Register Office marriages 31 per cent were the first marriage for both partners. With a rising divorce rate, the churches' attitudes to the re-marriage of divorced people in church (see Unit 10, pp. 28–29) is bound to have an effect on the number of marriages taking place in church.

(see Unit 10, pp. 28–29)

TEST YOURSELF ON FACTS

1. At what age can you marry without parental consent?
2. Name three basic elements in marriage.
3. What does 'monogamy' mean?

CHRISTIAN PERSPECTIVES

SUGGESTIONS FOR BIBLE STUDY
Gen. 1.27; 2.18   Mark 10.2–9

Christians believe that God is the giver of life and that in marriage ordinary men and women share his work of creation. They believe that the human need for relationships is part of God's plan and that sexuality is his gift.

Jesus spoke about marriage as a lifelong commitment and, according to the fourth gospel, was himself guest at a wedding when he saved the day by performing a miracle when the wine ran out (John 2.1–12).

The Christian marriage ceremony makes it clear that Christians believe that God is involved.

WHAT DO YOU THINK?

1. Does being married in church make any difference? Should a church wedding be available to people who never go to church?
2. Should a woman promise to obey her husband?
3. In what ways do the promises made at a wedding affect the marriage? Does religious belief have any influence on the development of a marriage?

The Church of England service (ASB 1980) begins with a preface in which the minister reminds those present that 'marriage is a gift of God in creation and a means of his grace, a holy mystery in which men and women become one flesh.'

Three reasons are given for marriage:

1. That husband and wife may comfort and help each other (i.e. companionship and support).
2. That with delight and tenderness they may know each other in love, and through the joy of their bodily union, may strengthen the union of their hearts and lives (i.e. each will *give* and *receive* love, thus building up the marriage through finding personal and mutual fulfilment).
3. That they may have children.

Reminding them of the seriousness of what they are doing the minister leads each in vows to the other.

> 'I, *N* take you, *N*,
> to be my wife/husband,
> to have and to hold
> from this day forward;
> for better, for worse,
> for richer, for poorer,
> in sickness and in health,
> to love and to cherish (or to love, cherish and worship/obey – the couple can choose)
> till death us do part,
> according to God's holy law;
> and this is my solemn vow.'

The ring is then given, or rings are exchanged, as a sign of love and faithfulness and the minister then pronounces the couple husband and wife. He joins their right hands together, using words of Jesus as he says, 'That which God has joined together, let no man divide.'

CHECK YOUR UNDERSTANDING

Match each of the Bible references to what is said in the preface to the marriage service and the words in which the couple are pronounced to be man and wife.

COURSEWORK

If possible use a tape recorder (otherwise take detailed notes) and interview three married couples (i) in their twenties or thirties, (ii) in their forties or fifties, (iii) pensioners. Find out what they regard as important for a successful marriage.
Prepare questions to put to them based on what you have learned about marriage. When you have finished, discuss your findings in class. Then write at length on 'Marriage in Britain in the late twentieth century'.

TO START YOU TALKING

1. Make a list of the advantages and disadvantages of having brothers and sisters. Make another list of the advantages and disadvantages of being an only child.

2. Which of these functions of the family do you consider most important?

(a) Having children
(b) Provision of a home
(c) Training children to cope with life
(d) Caring for all members of the family, including grandparents, who may or may not live nearby, the sick and the handicapped
(e) Providing religious training.

    Compare your answers with your neighbour's and then together decide whether any of these functions is performed more effectively by outside agencies such as Social Services, school or Church. Give reasons.

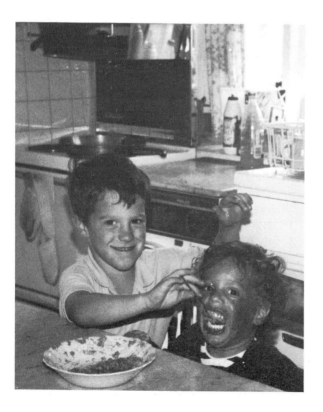

INFORMATION

1. PARENTHOOD

It has been said that children create adults not the other way round, i.e. the responsibilities of parenthood rapidly make people more mature. Try to imagine the shock of having a new baby in the house and realising that *you* are now Mum and Dad who are expected to know what to do in any crisis; *you* are the ones who are responsible for feeding, clothing, educating and above all *giving* love to this tiny scrap so that he/she will grow up into a responsible adult. Of course the experience will make you more mature, if you will allow it to.

Teenage parents

Some, especially teenage parents who regret the restrictions which responsibility brings, cannot rise to the challenge of the endless work a baby makes. The mother is tired out by the demands made on her. Her husband finds he is no longer the focus for all her love and that she is too tired to respond to him as she used to. They may well be restricted in income so that there is less money available for entertainment. They either share the joys and worries and grow together, each aware of the other's love and support in an undemanding way which deepens their own relationship or they become self-centred, looking for a way of escape. Thus is family life created or broken.

TEST YOURSELF ON FACTS

Score one point for each correct answer.

1. Name three functions of the family.

2. What do you understand by these terms applied to families?
   (a) extended,
   (b) nuclear,
   (c) reconstituted.

3. Give two advantages experienced by children in single parent families.

4. Name two problems experienced by single-parent families.

2. TYPES OF FAMILY

(a) Extended family

This was the usual pattern of family life until modern times in this country. Several generations live together or close enough to be available to help each other.

(b) Nuclear family

This is the pattern of family life in Britain today with natural parents and their children living as a separate unit. According to a report published in 1981 by the Study Commission on the Family, one-third of households are 'nuclear' families.

(c) Reconstituted ('step') family

Nearly one in five children will experience the divorce of their parents before they reach their sixteenth birthday and, since most people who divorce under the age of 30 re-marry within five years, many of those children will form part of 'reconstituted' families.

(d) One-parent families

About one in seven of all children live in one-parent families, which in 1985 made up 14 per cent of all families with dependent children.

Make two columns in your book headed 'Parents' and 'Children'. Copy out the following list of effects of belonging to a single-parent family putting each item in the column of the people most affected.

(i) It is necessary to make provision for the care of the child while the parent is at work.

(ii) Financial difficulties. The majority of women with dependent children who are receiving income support are separated or divorced wives and unmarried mothers.

(iii) The child is deprived of the influence of one parent.

(iv) There are extra presents for the children at Christmas and birthdays.

(v) Parents tend to treat their children as friends and equals.

(vi) The parent has to make difficult adjustments to parenthood unsupported by a husband/wife.

(vii) Unmarried mothers receive less sympathetic support than the widow or father coping with bringing up a child single-handed.

(viii) When parents are separated there are likely to be extra treats at the weekends and holidays with each parent.

(ix) There may be difficulty in finding suitable accommodation where the child will be welcome.

(x) The child sometimes has a choice of where to live.

Do the benefits of being in a single-parent family outweigh the disadvantages?

CHECK YOUR UNDERSTANDING

1. *Why do you think it is more difficult for teenage parents to build a family?*

2. *Can you account for the fact that the pattern of family life in this country has changed from the extended to the nuclear pattern?*

WHAT DO YOU THINK?

1. What part should grandparents play in family life?
2. In what ways can
   (a) the government,
   (b) the churches,
   (c) individuals, improve the quality of family life?

CHRISTIAN PERSPECTIVES

> **SUGGESTIONS FOR BIBLE STUDY**
> Ex. 20.12   Luke 15,11–32
> Mark 3.31–35   Eph. 5.33–6.4

Look up each of the Bible references for yourselves. Do not rely solely on the information which follows.

1. The Ten Commandments

Jesus was part of a human family and so Christians believe has given his blessing to family life. As a Jew Jesus would have tried to obey the commandment in Exodus 20.12. *Look it up.*

2. The Fatherhood of God

Jesus taught his followers to address God as Father. If the Creator is father, then *everyone* without exception is brother or sister. This belief will affect behaviour. For example, you may feel strongly that hanging should be re-introduced in cases of violent crime. Would you feel the same if you knew the criminal as your own brother or sister?

3. Parable of the Lost Son

In this parable of the prodigal son (*What does 'prodigal' mean?*), Jesus paints a picture of a loving father. *Read the story in Luke 15 and then read the following list of statements. Pick out those which are true and copy them into your books.*

(a) *The elder son asked the father to divide the property between the two sons.*
(b) *The younger son sold his share and went off with the money.*
(c) *The younger son wanted to buy some pigs of his own.*
(d) *Because the younger son was down and out he decided to swallow his pride and ask his father for a job.*
(e) *The father saw him coming and went out to meet the returning son because he loved him so much.*
(f) *He ordered a party to celebrate his son's return.*
(g) *The elder brother asked if he could join in.*
(h) *The elder brother was also in need of forgiveness (for what?) and the father wanted to forgive him too (what stood in the way?)*
(i) *The father's love was expressed in forgiveness.*

4. St Paul

St Paul offers plenty of advice on family life. Remember that expectations were very different in first century Palestine but what he says is still relevant.

Read Ephesians 5.33–6.4.
Does he suggest husbands should lord it over their wives?
Does he make the wife subservient to her husband?
Why, according to St Paul, should children obey their parents?
Does his advice on how fathers should treat their children make it easier to obey parents?
Can you summarise the advice in one word?

The word is at the heart of the Christian perspective on family life.

COURSEWORK

Find out which organisations exist in your own area to help people who are cut off from the support of families. These fulfil many of the functions of the extended family, e.g. Age Concern, Compassionate Friends, Cruse, Gingerbread Groups, MENCAP, PHAB clubs. Are there any voluntary service units for young people? What part do local churches play in helping people in need?

Write at length about the way in which your own community is helping with tasks formerly undertaken by the extended family. What can you yourself do to help? If you are already involved, describe what you are doing. If not, consider ways in which you could help.

TO START YOU TALKING

Check that you understand the difference between natural and artificial methods of birth control and their relative effectiveness. If necessary your teacher will arrange a lesson dealing with the subject.

1. To whom would you turn for advice about contraception — parents: doctor: family planning clinic: friends: other?
2. Is difficulty in obtaining sound advice the reason for unwanted pregnancies?
3. Is effective contraception responsible for the change in sexual morality?
4. Should Aid to the Third World be made conditional on a programme of contraception?

Mrs Victoria Gillick.

INFORMATION

1. CONTRACEPTION

(a) Reasons for contraception

Make two columns in your book headed Agree/Disagree. Copy the following list of reasons for using contraception into your book putting them into the appropriate column.

  (i) To limit the size of family.
 (ii) To space the children so that the mother does not become too tired through looking after them.
(iii) To relate the size of family to the size of income so that a reasonable standard of living can be maintained.
(iv) Because removing fear of unwanted pregnancy helps many couples to a relaxed enjoyment of their sexual relationship. This applies both within and outside marriage.

(b) The Gillick Judgement

The Gillick judgement established the legal position of people under the age of 16 who seek contraceptive advice from doctors. In 1984 Mrs Victoria Gillick, a mother with five daughters, took the Department of Health and Social Security to court over a circular to doctors which permitted them in certain circumstances to provide people under the age of 16 with contraceptive treatment without informing their parents. As parents are responsible for their children she felt they had a right to know if their children were seeking contraceptive advice. There was also a legal issue. As it is illegal for a man to have sexual intercourse with a girl under the age of 16 doctors were being put into the position of helping them to break the law. Mrs Gillick asked the court to declare that the advice in the circular was illegal. She lost her case in the first court, won in the Appeal Court but finally lost it in the House of Lords by three votes to two.

The most important argument considered by the Law Lords in favour of allowing doctors to give contraceptive advice to girls under 16 was that the parents' rights to control the behaviour of their children existed for the benefit of the *children*, not the parents and, since young people are often reluctant to talk to their parents about sexual matters, depriving them of professional advice was likely to lead to pregnancy rather than discouraging sexual activity.

Doctors are therefore now allowed in certain circumstances to provide contraceptive treatment for people under the age of 16 without having to inform parents.

The doctor must be satisfied that the girl understands what the advice means. He should also do his best to persuade her to talk to her parents or to allow him to tell them. If however she refuses and the doctor is of the opinion that her health will suffer unless she receives contraceptive advice, he is allowed to give her the necessary treatment without parental consent.

2. WORLD POPULATION

The population of the world is growing at a staggering rate. Every minute 150 babies are born. That is 220,000 every day or about 80 million in a year (*The Times*, 26 May 1987).

Draw a graph to illustrate the following figures of world population growth:

It took until 1830 for the world population to reach 1 billion. In another hundred years that figure had doubled to 2 billion. In another 45 years (i.e. 1974) it had doubled again to 4 billion. Only 13 years later it reached 5 billion (1987). By the year 2000 it is estimated it will have reached 6 billion (statistics source: *The Times*, 26 May 1987).

Nine out of ten babies are born in the Third World where poverty, disease and famine mean a high proportion will not survive. Because there is no social security system in these countries parents need to have large families to look after them when they are too old to work, so they do not take kindly to advice to limit the size of their families.

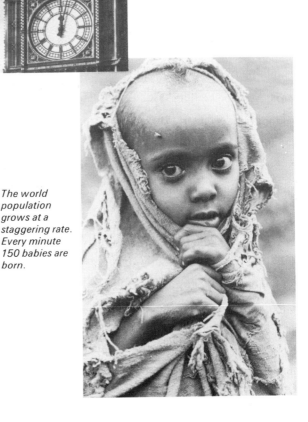

The world population grows at a staggering rate. Every minute 150 babies are born.

In Europe and the United States feeding the population is no problem but there is a declining death rate. We know everyone must die but improved medicine means people live longer so, world-wide, the population continues to grow.

CHECK YOUR UNDERSTANDING

1. *Give an account of the Gillick case explaining why Mrs Gillick took the DHSS to court and what the Law Lords decided. Explain why some people think that girls under 16 should be given contraceptive advice and why others oppose the idea. What do you think? Would you think differently (i) if you had five daughters, (ii) if you were a Roman Catholic?*

2. *Explain a basic difference between the Roman Catholic church and other churches in their approach to the fight against world poverty.*

WHAT DO YOU THINK?

Should people be forbidden to have more than a certain number of children? How could this be enforced? On the other hand, with an ageing population, are there disadvantages in discouraging parents from having large families?

TEST YOURSELF ON FACTS

1. Who is Mrs Victoria Gillick?
2. What was the world population in 1987?
3. What is it estimated it will be by the year 2000?
4. What proportion of all babies is born in the Third World?

CHRISTIAN PERSPECTIVES

1. CONTRACEPTION

Contraception is an issue over which Christians come to different conclusions. You have to make up your own minds, but here is some guidance from the churches.

(a) The Roman Catholic Church

A famous encyclical issued by Pope Pius VI in 1968 entitled *Humanae Vitae* upheld traditional Roman Catholic teaching that the sex act is designed for the procreation of children and that those who interfere with its natural power are doing something sinful. The Roman Catholic Church still opposes artificial means of birth control.

(b) The Church of England

A Church of England statement on birth control is contained in a report from the Lambeth Conference of 1958. It said that God had given the responsibility for deciding the number and frequency of children to parents and that parents should consult their own consciences and agree together, making a positive choice before God.

(c) The Free Churches

A typical attitude is that which appeared in the report from the General Assembly of the Church of Scotland in 1960. It emphasised that parenthood is a sacred responsibility which need no longer be haphazard since contraception makes it possible to control the number of children born so that their upbringing is within the strength of the mother and the family finances. This shows a *higher* regard for human life than leaving birth to chance.

True or False?

From the following statements, copy those which are true into your books.

(i) Roman Catholics are not allowed to use any form of birth control.

(ii) The Roman Catholic Church teaches that it is sinful to interfere artificially with procreation.

(iii) The Church of England says that parents can please themselves.

(iv) The Church of England says that parents should try to know what is God's will in their own situation.

(v) A Church of Scotland Report says that the

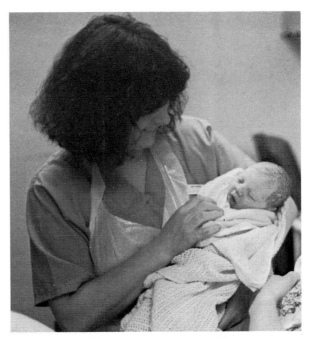

strength of the mother and the family finances are more important than having children.

(vi) A Church of Scotland Report says that human life is too important for procreation to be left to chance.

2. WORLD POPULATION

There is a clear link between poverty and population but, because of their differing views on contraception, Christians do not agree over what action to take. Because of its belief in the sinful nature of artificial means of birth control the Roman Catholic Church wants poverty in the over-populated areas of the world to be tackled through a redistribution of wealth rather than by contraception. Other churches, among them the Church of England, believe that the teaching of methods of birth control is an essential part of tackling the problem of world population.

COURSEWORK

Invite an outside speaker to talk to the class about contraception and then write a detailed report on the talk relating it to the moral issues discussed in this Unit.

21

UNIT 8   Communities

TO START YOU THINKING

Find out about a community in your own locality. If possible visit them; otherwise invite someone from the community to come and tell you about it. Use the following questions as the basis of your investigation:

(a) What brought the community together in the first place?
(b) What promises, if any, do its members make?
(c) How do they earn their living?
(d) Is this work the main purpose of the community? If not, what *is* its main purpose?
(e) What are the benefits/disadvantages for individual members in community life?

INFORMATION

1. KIBBUTZIM

Have you ever thought of working on a kibbutz (pl. kibbutzim)? There are about 250 kibbutzim in Israel varying in size from about 200 to 2000 people. What would you find if you did try kibbutz life? Several things would be likely to strike you, e.g.

(a) Money is unnecessary as all basic needs are provided.
(b) If individuals go outside the community to work, they do not keep their salaries but the money is paid into a central fund.
(c) People have individual rooms (or married quarters) but meals are eaten together in the communal dining room and everyone takes turns at the boring jobs like clearing away and washing up.
(d) Children are brought up together in children's houses and parents pop in to see them whenever

they can. In this way the extended family pattern is adopted (see Unit 6, p. 17) everyone taking an interest in the welfare of all the children.

> ### CHECK YOUR UNDERSTANDING
> 1. Why is money unnecessary on a kibbutz?
> 2. In what way is equality shown regardless of occupation?
> 3. Which pattern of family life is adopted?

Although originally based on working the land, kibbutzim also have factories. There is no financial difference between management and workers and no bonuses for doing the boring jobs.

> ### WHAT DO YOU THINK?
> 1. How do the boring jobs in a kibbutz get done? Why does this not happen outside such a community?
> 2. Discuss the advantages and disadvantages of children not being brought up by their own parents. In what ways does the method adopted in a kibbutz differ from boarding school?
> 3. What might be the problems of teenagers growing up in a kibbutz? Are they different from those experienced in the outside world?

2. MONASTERIES

Religious communities – monasteries and convents – still flourish in the twentieth century. There are two kinds:

(a) **Active communities** which have been founded with some specific work in mind, e.g. teaching, nursing, social work, missionary work.
(b) **Enclosed communities** which spend their lives in prayer and work – sometimes very hard work.

People sometimes say that this is a waste of a life as we are born into this world to help our fellowmen and to enjoy ourselves. *What do you think?* To some extent it depends on the way in which you understand prayer and the value you put on it.

An experiment
Each member of the class writes on a piece of paper how many minutes a week he/she spends in prayer. Count a school assembly as ten minutes. If you go to a place of worship, count the service as 1 hour. Add private prayer to the total. Collect the pieces of paper (they can be secret without folding them into tiny pieces!) and get someone who is quick

with a calculator to produce an average. How long is it per week/day? Monks and nuns would spend at least 8 hours a day in prayer.

Monastic vows

The traditional vows are poverty, chastity, obedience, although there are variations.

(a) *Poverty*

Poverty does not mean destitution. Even Mother Teresa and her sisters, who share the lives of the very poorest, are adequately fed. Nothing is gained by helpers becoming weakened through neglecting their own basic needs. Monastic poverty is more a matter of living simply, possessing nothing for one's own exclusive use.

(b) *Chastity*

The vow of chastity involves making a positive choice to remain unmarried. People sometimes imagine this choice has been forced on individuals through nobody wanting to marry them. This is by no means the case. Otherwise monastic communities would be places full of frustration rather than stable communities where visitors go to find peace. Freedom from the responsibilities of marriage leaves the monk or nun free to love and serve a wider community.

(c) *Obedience*

The vow of obedience means searching to obey God's will rather than blindly doing what a superior says, although obedience will of course involve co-operating with others for the good of the whole community.

An individual will have lived the life of a religious for 7–10 years, passing through various stages and learning exactly what the life involves, before taking final vows for life. *Now read about Br Roger and the Taizé community.* (p. 24).

Now read about Br Roger and the Taizé community. (p. 24).

TEST YOURSELF ON FACTS

1. What are the traditional monastic vows?
2. What is an 'enclosed' community?
3. Do kibbutzniks take vows?

CHRISTIAN PERSPECTIVES

SUGGESTIONS FOR BIBLE STUDY

Acts 2.44–46; 4.32–35
Romans 12.6–8
1 Corinth. 12.4–11

The idea of community life goes back to the earliest days of Christianity. It was an expression of the first Christians' 'common unity' of faith.

1. List the activities of the early church community mentioned in the Bible references in Acts. Which of them apply to the kinds of community described in this Unit?
2. List the gifts mentioned by St Paul in 1 Corinth. 12.4–11 through which Christians believe God's Spirit can be shown in the world. Does this passage help to make sense of devoting a whole life to prayer?

COURSEWORK

Try to spend a day (or longer) with a community and then write a letter to a friend describing the experience in detail and telling something about the purpose for which the community was founded.

Brother Roger of Taizé

Anyone driving near Cluny in France is likely to feel impelled to offer lifts to back-packing young people wending their way along country roads. Taizé is the magnet drawing them from every corner of the world to experience for themselves the sense of reconciliation which flows through the community for whom it is home. Reconciliation is the bringing together in love of people who have misunderstood each other.

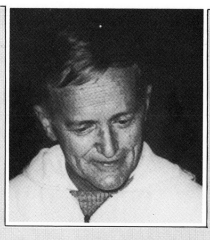

At the heart of Taizé is the vision of Brother Roger. He was born near Neuchâtel in Switzerland on 12 May 1915, the last of nine children and the only boy left in a household with seven sisters. His father was a Protestant pastor, an exceptionally tolerant man, and right from childhood young Roger was exposed to reconciliation in practice. He recalls how his maternal grandmother, a staunch protestant, when she had to leave Paris and live in the country, used to attend Roman Catholic Mass. He remembers too an occasion when his own father went openly into the Catholic church to pray. Even in a period when catholics and protestants distrusted each other, young Roger was learning to look beyond the prejudices and was coming to realise that the closer a person comes to God, the less the differences matter.

In his early teens he had to go away to school, which involved lodging in the town. Two families offered hospitality, one Protestant and the other Catholic. The Catholic family, with a widowed mother struggling to bring up numerous children, badly needed the money so, despite the religious difference, Roger's parents arranged for their son to live with her.

After leaving school and a period of illness during which he had serious doubts about his own faith, Roger went to Lausanne to study theology. By the end of his course Europe was at war and France, his mother's native land, had been defeated. At this stage the Germans occupied only part of the country, southern France coming under a puppet government set up at Vichy.

In August 1940 Roger crossed the border ostensibly to visit an uncle but really in search of a house where with others he could live the life of a religious. He wanted to provide a place of peace for people suffering through war and discouragement. Eventually he found a house in Taizé, a village north of Cluny. The key was kept by an old woman and, after visiting the house, Roger asked where he could get a meal. She invited him to share her own and he talked to her about his plans. She begged him to come there as they were poor, isolated and saddened by bad times. On his return to Switzerland his father encouraged him by pointing out that Christ is most readily found among the poor. Accordingly the following month Roger returned to Taizé and bought the house.

At first he lived alone, praying three times a day and learning to work the land. His first guests brought danger; many of them were refugees escaping from occupied France. He asked no questions but helped them on their way. Eventually he himself had to leave.

After the war, when he returned to Taizé with a few companions to continue the religious life there, he reached out in reconciliation to the enemy, sharing the community's meagre food with German prisoners brought over on Sundays from a neighbouring camp. His action angered villagers who had suffered at German hands and it was a long time before the generosity of the monastic community brought about reconciliation with these neighbours.

In 1949 the first seven brothers, took monastic vows for life. Today there are over eighty brothers, Catholics, and from various Protestant backgrounds. They are scattered across the world as 'signs of the presence of Christ among men, and bearers of joy'. Taizé fraternities are to be found in some of the world's worst slums.

All this time visitors continued to arrive in Taizé, particularly young people.

They could camp but, by the late nineteen fifties, the church was overflowing. The brothers themselves had no money to build another but a group of German Christians were moving around Europe building signs of reconciliation in places where people had suffered at German hands. They built the Church of Reconciliation for the community and it was dedicated in 1962. Eventually even this building became too small and walls were knocked down to allow a huge tent extension.

From now onwards Taizé was to become increasingly identified with young people. Of course all ages are welcomed but the community has shown particular understanding of those who are starting out on a life of faith.

A Pilgrimage of Trust on Earth

Those who return home after a stay at Taizé know they share their searching with many others. However they form no organised movement. Each person is called to become involved where they live and to be a person of reconciliation there. Local churches, as meeting points for a wide variety of people, can play an important role in this. It is possible to open little paths of reconciliation in one's own city or district by visiting persons, groups and communities to discover all their different gifts – it can become a lifelong pilgrimage.

As a visible sign of this widespread pilgrimage, meetings are held from time to time in large cities. All participants gather in city-centre cathedrals for common prayer with Brother Roger and the brothers of Taizé. They are welcomed by local churches, religious communities and families throughout the city and they make visits to places of hope.

Look out for news of these meetings and try to get to them. Quite often they are held in London. Those who share the vision of Taizé are to be like the yeast in a loaf of bread, living the life of Christ in their own communities and cracking the crustiness of set ways which have lost their vitality.

Find out more about Taizé for yourselves. Get hold of the cassette, Songs from Taizé, *and learn some of them yourselves. They are easy to sing and will give you an impression of the atmosphere of the place. Best of all, as soon as you are able, go to Taizé yourself. Details of coach travel from London to Taizé direct are available from St Peter's Coaches, 4 Penerley Road, London, SE6 2LQ, or write to Taizé: 71250, Taizé Community, France.*

UNIT 9 — Conflict within the Family

TO START YOU TALKING

1. *Work in groups of four*

(a) What are the signs that parents care about their children? Is it ever helpful for the young person to be able to say 'I dare not. Mum/Dad would kill me.'?

(b) Is it possible for parents and children to talk about the feelings which underlie parental anxieties about their children? Why?/Why not?

(c) At what age do you think parents should treat their children as equals? Why?

(d) At what stage do you think the young person is likely to recognise that parents need help in accepting their children's independence? How can they be helped?

2. *Work in pairs*

(a) When serious rows develop between husbands and wives, should they try to hide them from the children?

(b) Should parents who no longer love each other try to stick together 'for the sake of the children'?

(c) Is there anything children can do to help relationships between parents or is it wiser to keep out of the arguments?

INFORMATION

Many young people experience great unhappiness at home and some become cynical about their own chances of success in relationships. If this is your own experience, take heart. There are many people who have learned from their parents' mistakes and it is possible to emerge from a broken home and still to make a success of your own marriage when the time comes.

Since our emotional life begins in the family, what we experience at home will colour the way we react to other people. Disagreements are inevitable when human beings live closely together and, as we do not live in a vacuum, our behaviour always affects other people. Look at some common causes of conflict.

1. CONFLICT BETWEEN PARENTS AND TEENAGERS

The basic problem is often striking the right balance between dependence/independence as the young person reaches adulthood.

In which of the following problem areas would this be the case?

(a) Parental disapproval of their children's friends.
(b) Parental insistence on children being home at a particular time (or failure of parents to care whether their children are out late).
(c) Parents criticising the way their children spend money.
(d) Mothers 'competing' with daughters in making themselves attractive, i.e. parental envy.
(e) Fathers who are sexually attracted to their daughters.
(f) Over-ambitious parents driving their children too hard, i.e. pride.
(g) Parents who are so wrapped up in their own lives that they become indifferent to their children's needs, i.e. selfishness.

(h) Teenagers who have noisy parties and do not do their share of the chores, i.e. selfishness.
(i) Parents trying to relive their own youth through their children's lives, i.e. an inability to 'let go'.
(j) Parents not trusting their children over drink, drugs, sex.

Doubtless you can add to the list!

2. CONFLICT BETWEEN HUSBANDS AND WIVES

Here are some of the sources of conflict. *List them in order of seriousness putting the most serious first and avoidable problems at the end.*

(a) Money problems/Unemployment.
(b) Partners fall in love with someone else.
(c) Interests develop along very different lines.
(d) Separation — work taking one partner away for long periods.
(e) Withholding of sexual life on the part of either.
(f) Inability to tolerate each other's friends.
(g) Disagreements over the upbringing of children.
(h) Interference from in-laws.
(i) Lack of interest/understanding of the problems of each other's lives, e.g. husbands who become engrossed in their work and give little time to family life; wives who are either frustrated and bored by the demands of small children or exhausted by the effort of running both home and job.
(j) Personality difficulties, e.g. selfishness, intolerance, meanness.

Look at the avoidable problems. How would you deal with them if you were in that situation?

CHECK YOUR UNDERSTANDING

Here are some real life comments made by people involved in stressful situations at home. Bearing in mind the information contained in this Unit, what do you see as the underlying cause of conflict in each case?

1. 'Money doesn't grow on trees. That's all you're getting.'

2. 'Sharing the kitchen is the worst part. All Ma-in-law does is tell me she knows what her son likes and he won't like what I'm doing.'

3. 'They just don't trust me to get myself home from a party. How am I supposed to know what time it's going to end or who'll bring me home?'

4. 'I never interfere, of course, but it worries me to see them giving in to the child. He's not four yet but always gets his own way.'

5. 'It's all right for you. You just go off down the pub. I never get away from the kids. You don't love me any more.'

---

3. SOURCES OF HELP

It is necessary above all to have someone whose confidentiality can be trusted. Some people find it easier to talk over their problems with another member of the family. Some trust some teachers (it's true!). Some confide in ministers of religion. There are also many caring organisations to whom one can turn.

The Samaritans

(a) Samaritans

The local telephone number is in all telephone directories. Samaritans was founded in 1953 by the Revd Chad Varah, rector of St Stephen's Church, Walbrook, in the City of London. He discovered that three suicides were taking place in London each day and determined to do something to help. He publicised the church telephone number so that anyone in despair could have someone to talk to. People began to telephone — nowadays two and a quarter million do so every year — and some came to the church office. Chad Varah then noticed that people in trouble were helped by talking to voluntary workers who originally were simply making cups of tea and helping with clerical work. Sympathy and the ability really to *listen* are the hallmarks of Samaritans and today there are over 20,000 volunteers working round the clock in every part of the country. They work anonymously being known only by their first names and confidentiality is guaranteed. Some of the volunteers are teenagers; all are carefully selected and thoroughly trained. (*Is this something you could do?*)

Although their name comes from the well-known story of the Good Samaritan, by no means all of the volunteers are Christians and, if they are, they must not speak about their faith to embarrass clients.

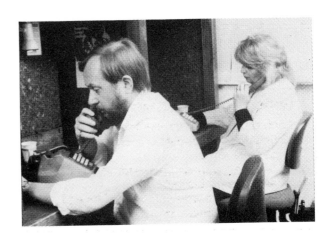

(b) Childline

The telephone number is 0800 1111 and professional counselling is available for young people in trouble or danger. This service began in 1987 as public concern grew over the question of child abuse and Esther Rantzen was able to mobilise the power of television to help.

(c) Citizens' Advice Bureaux

Although not primarily concerned with helping to resolve family difficulties, the CAB is manned by staff whose confidentiality can be trusted and they are aware of services in their own areas which could help. Find them through the telephone directory or look for notices in the public library.

(d) RELATE (Marriage Guidance Council)

Relate is concerned with all aspects of marriage, not just helping marriages in distress. It believes that happy family life forms the basis of society and affirms that marriage should be a partnership for life. It is involved in educational work as well as counselling when marriages are breaking down.

TEST YOURSELF ON FACTS
1. Who founded Samaritans?
2. What service is provided by Relate?
3. What is Childline?

WHAT DO YOU THINK?
Look at the situations listed in the Check Your Understanding box. Then answer these questions:
1. Is there a Christian perspective on any/ all of the problems?
2. What advice would you like to give to everybody involved in each situation?

CHRISTIAN PERSPECTIVES

SUGGESTIONS FOR BIBLE STUDY
Ex. 20.12	Matt. 5.21–24
Eph. 4.25–32; 5.33–6.4	Luke 15.11–32

St Paul in his letter to the Ephesians shows an astute understanding of how people react when they are irritated and thwarted. What does he mean by 'we are all members together in the body of Christ'?

From this letter and the other passages from the Bible listed in the box, you should be able to work out for yourselves the Christian perspective on conflict within the family. To help you, work out the answers to the following questions:

(i) Are any of the ten commandments relevant/ helpful?

(ii) According to the Sermon on the Mount, what does Jesus say is as serious as murder? Is this realistic?

(iii) What does St Paul say in Eph. 5.33–6.4 about the way in which Christians should behave towards each other?

(iv) Re-read the story of the prodigal son. What light does the story throw on conflict within the family and the way in which it can be resolved? There is an exercise on this parable in Unit 6 (p. 18) which will help you.

(v) Think of an occasion of family conflict in which you yourself were involved. Now re-read 1 Corinth. 13 and apply it to *yourself* in that situation. Could the conflict have been avoided if everyone involved had lived up to the standard set by St Paul? What prevents people from doing so?

COURSEWORK
Invite a speaker from one of the agencies mentioned in this Unit to come and talk to the class about its work. Then write a detailed report on what you learn.

TO START YOU TALKING

1. Work in groups of four

What do you think are the reasons for marriage breakdown? Is it possible to avoid them?

2. Work in pairs

What are the effects of divorce on (a) the couple, (b) the children, (c) others involved. Who are these others? There are more than you may at first think.

INFORMATION

Because people are living longer and are marrying younger, on average marriage can be expected to last for fifty years – twice as long as in the nineteenth century. But, in the words of Professor O. R. McGregor, (*Divorce in England*, Heinemann, 1957), 'the divorce courts are now called upon to deal with disputes formerly settled by the undertaker'.

What did he mean? Does his comment suggest that marriages were happier in the past?

As marriage is increasingly regarded as a personal matter and the influence of both Church and Society on the individual declines, it is almost inevitable that the divorce rate should rise.

(a) The Law

(i) Until 1969 divorce was only possible if a 'matrimonial offence' – adultery, cruelty, desertion or the wilful refusal of sex relations – had been committed.

(ii) *1969 Divorce Reform Act*
Under this current law the judge has to be satisfied that the marriage has irretrievably broken down (i.e. the sole ground of a 'matrimonial offence' is abandoned). When the Act was passed it required two years to elapse without the couple having lived in a state of marriage (five years if one partner objected to the divorce).

(iii) *1984 Matrimonial and Family Proceedings Act*
This Act now allows people to petition for divorce after only one year of marriage.

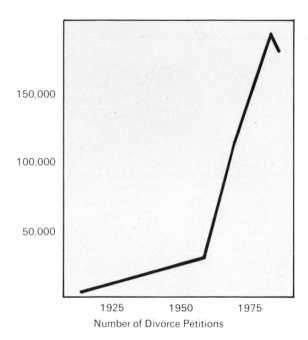

Number of Divorce Petitions

(b) Statistics

There has been almost a hundredfold increase in the number of divorce petitions per 10,000 married couples over a period of seventy-five years.

Draw a graph to illustrate the following figures:

Year	Total Number of Petitions	Number per 10,000 Couples
1911	902	1.38
1961	32,000	21
1971	111,000	60
1985	191,000	134
1988	183,000	128

1971 was the year in which the 1969 Divorce Reform Act became effective, which accounts for the enormous increase in the number of divorces in that year.

TEST YOURSELF ON FACTS

1. What is the main difference between the grounds for divorce up to 1969 and after that date?
2. How many divorce petitions were there in (a) 1911, (b) 1988?
3. Which age group has the highest divorce rate?
4. How many divorce petitions were there in 1971?

The 1985 figure of 191,000 divorce petitions represents an increase of 6 per cent over the 1984 total, but that was the year in which the Matrimonial and Family Proceedings Act became effective. *Why should this suddenly increase the number of divorces?*

Those who remarry after divorce are nearly twice as likely to divorce again. The younger the wife at marriage the greater the chance of divorce. The proportion of teenage marriages ending in divorce is twice that of those who marry between the ages of 20 and 24.

CHRISTIAN PERSPECTIVES

SUGGESTIONS FOR BIBLE STUDY
Matt. 5.31–32; 19.1–12
1 Corinth. 7.10–11

1. DIVORCE

The Church is bound to uphold the teaching of Jesus that marriage is for life but equally it has a duty to support and comfort those suffering from marriage breakdown.

Do you think the demands of love (and therefore of God) require two people whose love for each other is dead to continue living together unhappily, with all the misery that is bound to spill over on to those around them, especially the children?

(a) St Matthew

St Matthew's version of Jesus' teaching suggests that this was a problem for the earliest Christians too. Matthew includes an 'exception clause' (Matt. 5.31–32). *What does it say?* Scholars think this was the way the first Christians coped with a situation where one partner was persistently unfaithful, leaving the other partner little choice but to let go.

(b) St Paul

What does St Paul tell Christians in Corinth to do in the matter of divorce? Notice that he emphasises that this is Christ's teaching and not merely his own.

(c) Putting Asunder

In 1968 a commission appointed by the Archbishop of Canterbury published its findings on the subject of marriage breakdown, under the title *Putting Asunder.* Its main conclusion was that there should be only one ground for divorce, the irretrievable breakdown of the marriage. This was incorporated into the 1969 Divorce Reform Act. *Putting Asunder* describes divorce thus, (It is) 'not a victory for one spouse and a reverse for the other; but a defeat for both, a failure of the marital "two in oneship" in which both its members, however unequal their responsibility, are inevitably involved together.'

2. REMARRIAGE

The moral problem for Christians arises not so much with desertion, separation or divorce – the three ways in which marriages effectively cease to exist – as with the problem of whether or not marriage is a repeatable ceremony.

Can anyone promise 'till death us do part' knowing that a previous spouse is still alive?

(a) The Lichfield Report

In 1979 the Church of England published a report, *Marriage and the Church's Task,* which had been prepared by a commission led by the Bishop of Lichfield. It set out both sides of the argument over the remarriage of divorced people in church.

Divide a page of your books into two, headed 'For' and 'Against' and copy out the following arguments from the Lichfield Report under the appropriate heading.

(i) Although marriage is for life, there is no denying the *fact* of marriage breakdown.

(ii) It is difficult for the Church to uphold Christ's teaching on marriage if it is seen to allow re-marriage after divorce.

(iii) An increasing number of all marriages, including those of people marrying for the first time, involve divorced persons, so fewer people have the opportunity of a 'church' wedding.

(iv) A refusal to allow remarriage in church gives the impression that marriage breakdown is an unforgiveable sin which is a denial of the gospel of forgiveness.

(v) Any attempt to differentiate between 'innocent' parties in a divorce and others involves judgements which belong to God alone.

The *Lichfield Report* summarised the problem thus: 'the task facing the Church is to fashion a discipline which holds before those who are married, and those about to marry, the challenge of unconditional love, while offering to those who have failed in their marriage the possibility of a new beginning.'

(b) Church of England

The present position in the Church of England is that under the law of the land a parish priest has the right to marry in church people who have been divorced but the Church itself strongly discourages his doing so — an example of something which is legal not necessarily being right in the eyes of the Church. The usual procedure is for such a marriage to take place in a Register Office and then be followed by a service of prayer and dedication either in church or at home.

(c) Orthodox Churches

Orthodox churches take the view that *marriages* die as well as people. If this happens the marriage ceases to exist and a second marriage can then be solemnised.

(d) The Free Churches

These in effect follow a course similar to the Orthodox.

(e) Roman Catholic Church

Catholics do not recognise divorce but have their own special nullity procedure which is described in the next section.

WHAT DO YOU THINK?

Does a knowledge of Christian teaching help people to cope with the problems which divorce brings? What are these problems?

CHECK YOUR UNDERSTANDING

1. Can you account for the great increase in the number of divorces in 1971?

2. Write two sentences to show the Church's duties in the area of divorce.

3. Write a paragraph explaining why the Church is reluctant to remarry 'innocent' parties to a divorce.

4. Write an essay explaining arguments for and against the Church allowing the marriage of divorced people in church.

3. NULLITY

It is open to the courts to pronounce a marriage null in certain circumstances. For example a bigamous 'marriage' (= where one partner is already married to someone else) is not a marriage; nor is a 'marriage' where one partner refuses sexual relations. This is a matter of the law.

From a religious point of view, the Roman Catholic Church, which does not recognise divorce, has its own courts which are empowered to declare marriages null from the Church's point of view. This is based on the belief that in some cases the cause of the breakdown was present at the outset of the marriage in the attitude or character of one of the partners. For example, if it could be shown that one partner had no intention of remaining loyal to the other at the outset of marriage, the requirement of personal loyalty would be lacking in the marriage and there would be a case for requesting a declaration of nullity from the Church's point of view. This is not an alternative to the *legal* requirement of obtaining a divorce before marrying someone else but enables Roman Catholics, in certain circumstances, to remarry. Respect for the system requires a Catholic understanding of marriage and it would be difficult to operate without such an understanding.

COURSEWORK

Invite a solicitor to come and talk to the class about divorce and the human problems involved. Then write a report on what you have learned.

TO START YOU TALKING

1. At what age is it appropriate to call someone old? (*Make a careful assessment of your teacher's age and be tactful!*) Why do people shy away from being called old?

2. In some countries the elderly are respected for their wisdom and experience. Can you account for the fact that this does not appear to be the case in this country?

INFORMATION

1. STATISTICS

More people in Britain are surviving to old age, partly because of an increase in the standard of living and partly because of improvements in modern medicine.

Year	Number of Age 65 +	Percentage of Total Population
1901	1.5 million	5
1966	6 million	12
1988	8.9 million	15(+)

Of people aged 65 or over, 52 per cent live in a household with their spouse, 36 per cent live alone and 7 per cent live with children or children-in-law.

Discuss your own experiences of caring for elderly relatives. Do they live in the kind of household they would prefer?

2. PROBLEMS OF OLD AGE

(a) **Financial difficulties**

Seven-tenths of pensioners depend on the state for their main income. The older people become, the smaller their incomes are likely to be; single and widowed women are the worst off.

Find out the weekly rate of state pension for (i) a single person, (ii) a married couple, (iii) a widow. What are the maximum savings a person may hold and still be eligible for income support?

(b) **Failing health**

Most elderly people accept health problems philosophically. The majority are not so handicapped that they could not stay in their own homes if adequate domestic help were available. The care of the elderly places a strain on the nuclear family (Unit 6, p. 17) but in Homes they become isolated from both their families and from society as a whole, and the loss of privacy contributes to a gradual loss of personal identity.

What services are available for the elderly in your own locality? Which of these are provided by the local authority and which by voluntary bodies?

(c) **Loneliness**

In 1985 almost half of women aged 65 + lived alone as against one-fifth of men of the same age. In previous generations the extended family (Unit 6, p. 17) would have taken care of them but now marriage or employment may well take the younger generation to other parts of the country or, indeed, the old people may retire to the country or coast. Living alone need not of itself produce loneliness but social isolation — i.e. not having friends to visit or friends to pop in for a chat — is a cause of much unhappiness. Bereavement, being housebound or being disabled bring a sense of isolation from the community.

TEST YOURSELF ON FACTS

1. Give two reasons for there being an increasing number of old people.
2. What percentage of the total population is aged 65 + ?
3. What percentage of those lives alone?
4. What is the 'Golden Rule'?

(d) Feeling unwanted

No longer respected for their experience, many elderly people feel they have nothing to contribute to society and a sense of uselessness can lead to boredom.

(e) Awareness of approaching death

Although it is probably true to say that fear of death diminishes with age, it is nonetheless depressing to have friends and contemporaries dying.

CHRISTIAN PERSPECTIVES

1. On the treatment of the elderly

The Bible has little to say addressed specifically to the problems of old age as we see them. St Paul writes to Timothy with advice on the care of widows. *How does he tell the younger man to treat them?*

In a society based on the extended family pattern many of the problems faced by the elderly in twentieth century Britain would not have arisen. Nevertheless Christians take to heart the 'Golden Rule' expressed by Jesus in Matt. 7.12. Jesus did not invent the advice. The ten commandments make clear people's obligation to their parents and this advice was worked out in detail in the law of the Pharisees. Jesus criticised laws which made it possible for a man to side-step his obligation to his parents by giving all his money to the Temple (Mark 7.9–13) and, bearing in mind Christian teaching on love, the elderly should have nothing to fear in a society which professes to be based on Christian principles.

2. Christian perspectives of the elderly themselves

At the age of 52 the poet Robert Browning (who was to live to the age of 77) wrote a poem, *Rabbi Ben Ezra*, expressing a robust religious view of the ageing process. It is too long to quote in full but here is the first verse.

> Grow old along with me!
> The best is yet to be,
> The last of life, for which the first was made;
> Our times are in His hand
> Who saith 'A whole I planned,
> Youth shows but half; trust God; see all, nor be afraid!'

(*What does he mean by 'The last of life for which the first was made'?*)

Write down the thoughts of such a person when, finally widowed and unable to care for himself, he is about to be admitted to an Old People's Home.

UNIT 12 — Control of Death. Euthanasia

TO START YOU TALKING

1. If doctors and your relatives knew you were dying, would you want to be told?

2. Do I have the right to decide when my own life should end? Is it reasonable to expect someone else to end it for me?

3. Are we justified in spending large sums of money in saving the life of one elderly person? Would you feel differently if that person were your own mother or brother?

INFORMATION

1. CONTROL OF DEATH

In a much publicised case about twenty years ago a BBC TV producer, preparing a programme in a hospital, came across a list of patients showing which of them should be given resuscitation in the event of collapse and which of them should be allowed to die. This problem of medical ethics is one in which any sick person might unwittingly be involved. Does it make any difference morally whether the patient is a young man critically ill after an accident or an elderly person paralysed by a stroke? What is a hopeless case? Who is to decide?

CHECK YOUR UNDERSTANDING

1. Why was there shock at the news that a hospital had a list showing which patients should be saved and which left to die?

2. What is the meaning of 'aid, abet, counsel or procure' as used in the 1961 Suicide Bill?

---

2. EUTHANASIA

It is one small step from failing to use every effort to keep a patient alive to taking steps actively to hasten death. Until 1961 it was a criminal offence to take one's own life — a fact which was unlikely to worry the person who succeeded but which had unpleasant consequences for those who failed in suicide attempts. The 1961 Suicide Bill removed the criminal stigma from suicide but it is still an offence to 'aid, abet, counsel or procure' such an act. Therefore a doctor may not help a patient to take his own life.

Every few years attempts are made to change the law and these have the support of such groups as the National Council for Civil Liberties, the British Humanist Association and the National Secular Society. The Voluntary Euthanasia Society (EXIT) publishes a booklet entitled *A Guide to Self-Deliverance* which tells people how they can take their *own* lives but so far parliament has not approved schemes to legalise voluntary euthanasia.

TEST YOURSELF ON FACTS

1. What is euthanasia?
2. What was the main clause of the 1961 Suicide Bill?
3. What is EXIT?

Doctors on the whole are opposed to euthanasia. Theirs is a healing profession and they are unwilling to become involved in the taking of life.

Would you have confidence going to a doctor who had the reputation of being sympathetic to euthanasia? What effect might it have on patients going into hospital if they knew doctors could decide whether it was worthwhile to make every effort to save them?

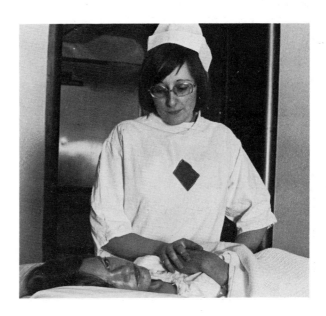

CHRISTIAN PERSPECTIVES

SUGGESTIONS FOR BIBLE STUDY
Gen. 2.4–3.21: 4.1–9
Luke 12.6–7

WHAT DO YOU THINK?

1. Would you be prepared to switch off a machine which was keeping an old person alive?
2. If it were legal, would you sign a document authorising someone to administer euthanasia to you yourself at some future date if it seemed unlikely you would recover from an illness or accident?

True or false?

Look up the Bible references in the box and then copy the statements which are true and match what you have found in the Bible texts. Write the Bible references beside the statements.

1. Life comes from God.
2. Life belongs to the individual and he can do what he likes with it.
3. God has a purpose for each individual.
4. Individuals are free to choose whether or not to obey God.
5. God cares more for sparrows than humans.
6. Every life is infinitely precious to God.

Christians are left facing two awkward questions:

(a) Is it sinful or merciful to release someone dying in misery?
(b) If it is for God alone to decide whether we should live or die, are we not 'playing God' just as much by healing people as by hastening death?

Organise a debate on the motion 'This House believes that an adult should be allowed to decide whether to end his/her own life.

Pope Paul VI summed up one Christian position in these words, (Euthanasia is) 'a temptation, in effect, to take the life of a man under the false pretext of giving him a pleasant and quiet death so as not to see him continue a hopeless life of atrocious agony. Without the consent of the person euthanasia is murder. His consent would make it suicide. Morally this is a crime which cannot become legal by any means.'

Other churchmen disagree, arguing that God has given us the capacity to reason and we should use that reason to the best of our ability. Churchmen are the ones who constantly visit the dying and even they come to different conclusions. For most of us outside the medical profession these issues only confront us when we are emotionally involved in the decisions and at such times it is difficult to think straight. *Now* is the time to make up your own minds while, it is hoped, the issue is not a personal one. Before deciding, read about the work of Dame Cicely Saunders and the Hospice movement (see opposite page). She is very much opposed to euthanasia, and the control of pain which has been achieved in hospices is one of the strongest medical arguments against changing the law.

COURSEWORK

Find out what provision is made in your area for the terminally ill. Perhaps there is a hospice; perhaps specialist nurses care for patients in their own homes. Invite a speaker to come and tell you about their work.

Ask what you can do to support their work and take appropriate action.

Then write a report on what you have learned explaining the ethical problem and expressing your own personal view at the end.

Part of the Helen Hospice for terminally ill children, Oxford.

Dame Cicely Saunders

No study of the problems of suffering and death is complete without some knowledge of the work of Dame Cicely Saunders. She was born in 1918 into a family which was, on the surface at least, privileged but she had a sad childhood. She was unhappy at school, her parents separated and her happiness when she began training as a nurse ended in disappointment when she had to give up because of back trouble. She switched to medical social work (in those days being known as a 'lady almoner') and completed training for this second career.

At the age of 29 she found herself with professional responsibility for a Pole who was dying of cancer. His name was David Tasma. He worked as a waiter, had no relations in this country and few friends. They fell in love. As they talked Cicely came to realise the acute need for deeper caring for the dying. Too often hospitals and doctors turned aside from dying patients, perhaps to shield themselves from the pain of having failed to cure them. She began to wonder whether an environment where the individual could be cared for as a *person*, with spiritual as well as physical and social needs taken care of, would enable more people to die in peace. As she and David discussed her ideas he began to find meaning and purpose for his own remaining life and death. In his will he left her £500 saying 'I'll be a window in your Home'.

She was advised that she would need to become a doctor if she wanted her views to be taken seriously and so, at the age of thirty-three, she began the long, hard training for her third profession. This was followed by a research fellowship which enabled her to study the control of pain in the dying which has become a cornerstone of Hospice care.

During this period of her life Cicely began to help at St Joseph's Hospice in Hackney, East London, which is run by Roman Catholic nuns. She met and talked to many dying patients and from them learnt of many of their problems and fears. She discussed her ideas with them and one of them, Barbara Galton, known to everyone as Mrs G., suggested a name. The dying are travellers to an unknown country. The Hospice should be named after the patron saint of travellers, St Christopher.

The turning point came on Midsummer Day in 1959. Cicely, who was by now a practising Christian, was reading the passage of the Bible appointed for that day. It was Psalm 37 which includes the words, 'Commit thy way unto the Lord; trust also in him; and he will bring it to pass.' The words seemed to jump off the page with special meaning for her own situation and she knew, beyond any shadow of doubt, that now was the time to act.

She put down her ideas on paper and sent copies to a number of influential people and gradually plans took shape.

At the height of so much activity, Cicely again fell in love with a dying patient, another Pole called Antoni Michniewicz. Shared Christian faith brought them together with heightened intensity in a relationship which flowered in the last three weeks of Antoni's life. His death left her desolate but with a fresh vision of the spirit which she wished to permeate St Christopher's. She had learnt that, in a relationship with people, even when one of them is dying, there is giving on both sides. She had also learnt that the last weeks of a patient's life can be the richest. Control of pain makes it possible for a person to be himself and really to live until the time of death. And she had come to believe through her own grief that the presence of God can be experienced even in the pain of parting. The pain of parting was to be renewed. Early the following year both her father and Mrs G., the friend who had suggested the name St Christopher's, died. Cicely had almost reached the end of her tether; it was as though she herself had to experience the kinds of sorrow which those she was to help would have to go through. Medical qualifications alone would be insufficient. She was to be provided with experiences which qualified her in every way as a human being to help the dying and the bereaved.

Then came the practical problems of fund raising and planning. She gathered around her many influential people and directed operations herself. Finally, in July 1967, the first patients arrived and the following week Princess Alexandra performed the opening ceremony. It was nearly twenty years since she had first talked over her ideas with David Tasma and now the opening of St Christopher's was to mark the beginning of a new phase in the treatment of the dying. Dame Cicely Saunders has made those who care for them aware that meeting medical needs alone is not enough. She has highlighted the need to control pain but has also shown that where the *whole* person is cared for – body, mind and spirit – the quality of the patient's remaining life is greatly enriched, bringing relief and comfort not only to the patient but also to the whole family. The quality of life found in hospices has become the most telling argument against euthanasia.

One happy personal footnote. In 1980 Dame Cicely bought a picture by the Polish artist Marian Bohusz-Szyszko. It was 'Christ calming the waters' and was to hang in the chapel at St Christopher's. She wrote to tell the artist of her excitement at the inspiration in his work. They met, fell in love and eventually married. A life story with a golden ending – a phrase which surely sums up her own life's work.

UNIT 13 | Life after death

TO START YOU TALKING

Which of these opinions come closest to your own?

1. I'd rather not think about death. It scares me stiff.
2. Death is the end. Your body is disposed of and that's that.
3. I think I shall come alive again as someone else.
4. This life is pointless if death is the end.
5. If you're good in this life you go to heaven when you die.
6. I don't believe in pie in the sky. It's just wishful thinking.
7. Astronauts would have found heaven if it existed.
8. Hell is horrible. You burn forever.
9. Dead people turn into ghosts and haunt us.
10. 'Life is not much to lose – but young men think it is.'

INFORMATION

Burial customs seem to indicate that from earliest times people have believed in life after death.

Ancient Egyptians
The pyramids were tombs for the pharoahs. The body was embalmed and provisions of all kinds were buried with it for use in the next life.

Reincarnation
Belief that after death a person is reborn in this life in a new body is found in such Eastern religions as Buddhism and Hinduism. According to this belief a person returns again and again to this world until the soul is freed from selfish desires.

Spiritualism
Spiritualists believe that it is possible to communicate with the dead, a practice which is regarded by Christians as open to fraud and potentially damaging.

Humanists
Humanists reject the idea of immortality as superstition and belief in life after death as an expression of a fear of death. They believe that human beings are descended from animals and that death is the end.

WHAT DO YOU THINK?
Does belief in an after life affect behaviour in this life?

CHRISTIAN PERSPECTIVES

SUGGESTIONS FOR BIBLE STUDY
Matt. 25.31–46   John 14.1–3
Luke 23.43   1 Corinth. 15.12–17

Christians speak of the 'four last things' (i.e. death, judgement, hell and heaven), and believe that the relationship they have formed with God in this life continues beyond the grave. They believe Jesus to be the first of a *new* creation, i.e. at his resurrection he was not merely resuscitated but changed, though still recognisably the same person. What happened to Jesus they believe will happen to them.

1. DEATH

At a Christian funeral mourning is expressed in the context of faith in the resurrection. As the coffin is brought into the church the minister speaks words from John 11.25–26 'Jesus said, "I am the resurrection, and I am the life; he who believes in me, though he die, yet shall he live, and whoever lives and believes in me shall never die".' At the moment of burial or cremation, according to the Church of England service (ASB) the minister says: 'We have entrusted our *brother N* to God's merciful keeping, and we now commit *his* body to the ground (*or* to be cremated): earth to earth, ashes to ashes, dust to dust: in sure and certain hope of the resurrection to eternal life through our Lord Jesus Christ, who died, was buried, and rose again for us. To him be glory for ever and ever.'

Thus Christians affirm their faith in life beyond death.

2. JUDGEMENT

The Bible teaches that people will be judged on their behaviour in this life and the standard Christians are set is the life of Christ – 'Be ye perfect'.

Read Jesus' parable of judgement in Matt. 25.31–45, noting that it is a story and NOT a guidebook to the hereafter.

'I've just had another near miss!'

TEST YOURSELF ON FACTS

1. What are the four last things?
2. In the parable of the sheep and goats list six things which the righteous have done.
3. What did the king say to the unrighteous?
4. Whom had they failed to serve?

Judgement is seen as a continuous process already taking place in every moment of this life since the way in which Christians behave either increases or diminishes the life of God within them so that they are continually either growing closer to God or are turning away from him.

3. HELL

Hell is being cut off from God. Christians believe that people *put themselves* there by turning their backs on God and ignoring the signposts to heaven. The imagery of everlasting flames is associated with Gehenna. This was the rubbish dump west of Jerusalem where fire was constantly burning. Because it was outside the holy city, Jerusalem, it became an image for a place cut off from God, whose presence was with his people in the holy city. In Jewish imagination, therefore, the things associated with a rubbish dump – everlasting fire and worms – became associated with being cut off from God.

CHECK YOUR UNDERSTANDING

1. *Why is the resurrection of Jesus central to Christian faith?*
2. *What do you understand by Gehenna?*
3. *What is Purgatory?*

---

4. HEAVEN

Heaven to Christians is being in the presence of God. Admittedly the imagery used to describe heaven is not very attractive to matter-of-fact people in the twentieth century. We tend to feel that, if we ever get there, we shall need an occasional holiday. But remember it is *imagery* not geography. The writers were trying to express the inexpressible. After all, if you were an acorn, how could you imagine what would happen to you once you had died and been born to new life? Yet, because the seed of that fully-grown oak tree is inside the acorn it would not be surprising if it had some intuition of what lay ahead.

5. PURGATORY

Some Christians feel they will not be ready at death to join the whole company of heaven. They believe there must be some intermediate stage to prepare people and, if this life is anything to go by, the process of having the remaining corners knocked off is likely to be painful. C. S. Lewis puts it like this:

'Our souls *demand* Purgatory, don't they? Would it not break the heart if God said to us, "It is true, my son, that your breath smells and your rags drip with mud and slime, but we are all charitable here and no one will upbraid you with these things, nor draw away from you. Enter into the joy"? Should we not reply, "With submission, sir, and if there is no objection, I'd *rather* be cleaned first." "It may hurt, you know" – "Even so, sir." ' (*Letters to Malcolm: Chiefly on Prayer*)

Other Christians believe that, as Jesus Christ has already done what they could never do for themselves – redeemed them (i.e., paid the price to free a slave) through his own death – nothing further is necessary.

6. ETERNAL LIFE

To Christians eternal life is not something which happens *beyond* death. Because of their faith in the Incarnation (i.e. that God became man in Jesus), Christians believe that the life of God is already present in the world and that the relationship they have formed with God in this life continues beyond the grave. They believe that those who have put their trust in Jesus *have* eternal life here and now.

COURSEWORK

1. Investigate the expression of Christian beliefs about life after death in art and architecture.
2. Investigate how C. S. Lewis expresses Christian beliefs about a world beyond this one in his *Narnia* books.

In either case write extensively about your findings.

TO START YOU THINKING

Make a chart in three columns using the following headings: (i) Cause of suffering, (ii) Nature of evil, (iii) Responsibility. In the first column write down the following causes of suffering:

Drunken driving: racial prejudice: child abuse: starvation in the Third World: crimes of violence: AIDS: hurricanes: gossip and its effect on all concerned: toothache: examinations failed through laziness: war and conflict in many parts of the world: a hangover: floods: slums in our cities: earthquakes.

In the second column decide whether the suffering is the result of natural or moral evil and mark it 'N' or 'M' accordingly.

For the third column make up your mind whether the responsibility is a personal one ('P'), one for which society is responsible ('S'), or whether those who suffer are innocent ('I').

WHAT DO YOU THINK?

1. If God is both loving and all-powerful, why does he not intervene to stop suffering?
2. Is suffering sent by God as a punishment?

Croydon rail disaster, 1988.

INFORMATION

You need to consider four aspects of suffering.

1. Suffering caused by moral evil in society

Look at your chart. Can God be blamed for any of the examples of social evils? Is it reasonable to blame him for not intervening to save innocent suffering in any of these situations which are caused by man's inhumanity to man? What would be the effect on human behaviour if he did?

2. Suffering caused by personal moral failure

Look at your chart. Can God be blamed for any of the suffering of this kind? Can you suggest why God allows people to behave in these ways? What would be the effect of removing our freedom to do wrong?

3. Suffering due to natural causes

(a) Some pain can be good – a warning sign. Toothache sends us to the dentist; a hangover makes us more careful next time.
(b) What about natural disasters – floods, earthquakes, hurricanes? How can a loving God allow such things to happen? Even here people often bear some responsibility. Much is now known about earthquakes yet cities are still built in areas where it is known they will occur one day. San Francisco is a case in point.
(c) We are left with hard cases which defy laying responsibility on ourselves, for example babies born with various handicaps.

4. Suffering as a mystery

Because we react to suffering with our emotions, we are unlikely to be satisfied with a purely reasoned response as we grapple with the problem. Yet anyone who refers to the 'mystery' of suffering is likely to meet superior smiles in those who think they are trying to dodge the issue. They aren't. The word 'mystery' describes the very nature of human life. We are all affected by many things which we can neither influence nor understand. In this sense suffering is as much part of living as the air we breathe. Joy and goodness are 'mysteries' too. We all experience them but we do not pretend to understand them, although it is part of being human to respond.

CHRISTIAN PERSPECTIVES

Christians have to confront the problem of having faith in a loving God who allows suffering. They find insights in three places:

> **SUGGESTIONS FOR BIBLE STUDY**
> John 9   Job 38 *et seq.*

1. The reactions of Jesus

In the fourth gospel we are told about an encounter which Jesus had with a man born blind (John 9). *Read the story for yourselves,* noticing especially that Jesus *healed* the man (as he did many other people during his ministry) i.e. he did not pretend that the suffering was good in itself. *In v.3 how does Jesus answer the suggestion that the man's blindness is God's punishment for sin?*

Christians would therefore find it wrong to make such comments as 'Why should something so terrible happen to her? She's such a nice person', since the implication is that suffering is a punishment for bad behaviour, that it is all right for cancer to strike a man who beats his wife every night or for a homosexual to contract AIDS. That is not God's way.

> **TEST YOURSELF ON FACTS**
> 1. Name three kinds of suffering caused by sins of society.
> 2. Name three kinds of suffering caused by personal sin.
> 3. Give three examples of pain which has an obvious purpose.
> 4. What did Jesus do for the man born blind?

2. Vicarious suffering

Vicarious suffering is suffering accepted on behalf of someone else. Christians believe that God's way is to set the mystery of his love right in the centre of the dark mystery of suffering. Jesus showed through his crucifixion and resurrection that love is stronger than evil and death. This may not seem a very practical 'explanation' of the problem of suffering but it provides a possible key to understanding the mystery of life within which we all live. Love overcomes evil.

Consider how the sight of suffering draws out the best in people. Think for yourselves of any local or personal tragedy which has led people to show great kindness to one another. We begin to see then that suffering need not be entirely negative in its effects. The power of love is greater.

3. The Book of Job (*say Jobe*)

The Old Testament contains a book which tackles the problem of innocent suffering. Job is an imaginary man to whom life has been kind. He is a good person, the head of a large family and the richest man in the East. Suddenly he loses everything – money, possessions, children. Then he himself suffers a horrible skin disease. Three friends visit him to bring him 'comfort'. They tell him he must have sinned to receive such a terrible punishment since God is just. Job knows he does not deserve such treatment and eventually challenges God to explain himself. He says the suffering would be easier to bear if he could understand the reason for it.

God does not answer Job's questions in the way he would like but instead gives him an overwhelming experience of God's wisdom and power. In a passage of magnificent poetry we see Job glimpsing God's majesty. It is worth reading some of it for yourselves. It starts at Chapter 38. Then Job realises that he cannot understand God's secrets and learns to trust him. Through *accepting* undeserved suffering rather than fighting against it he finds peace. The story is rounded off with a happy ending but the most important part of the book is Job's acceptance of the fact that he cannot *understand* God's ways but, in accepting them in trust, he finds peace.

> **CHECK YOUR UNDERSTANDING**
> 1. Write sentences to explain the meaning of 'vicarious suffering' and 'Job's comforters'.
> 2. Write a paragraph replying to someone who claims suffering is a punishment from God.

> **COURSEWORK**
> How many organisations can you find in your own locality devoted to the relief of suffering? Which of these uses voluntary workers? Choose one of them and investigate the following:
>
> 1. The history of the organisation.
> 2. The extent of its work in your own locality.
> 3. What difficulties are experienced by its workers and what has led them to help with the work.
> 4. How you yourself can help.
>
> Then write a report on your findings.

UNIT 15 — Addiction

TO START YOU TALKING

1. Should the law intervene to save people from killing themselves through smoking, drink or drugs?

2. Here are some reasons for people taking drugs. Discuss whether they are good reasons.
   Relief of pain: relief of stress and tension: relief of boredom: for fun and to be one of the crowd: to overcome shyness: to ease the pain of broken relationships: to overcome sleeplessness: to draw attention to oneself: to seek mystical experience: to stay awake to study before examinations.

INFORMATION

Drugs can mean anything from cigarettes and alcohol to cocaine and heroin. Even caffeine, which is freely available in coffee and tea is a stimulant — one used by millions of workers to keep themselves going between breakfast and their next meal. The heroin addict is, superficially at least, in a worse state than the chain smoker but neither of them is able to break the habit without considerable determination and both are likely to die if they continue.

1. THE LAW

(a) **Tobacco**
   (i) It is illegal to sell tobacco to anyone under 16.
   (ii) Advertisements must carry a health warning.
   (iii) Local bye-laws restrict smoking in certain public places.

(b) **Alcohol**
   (i) It is an offence to give alcohol to a child under 5.
   (ii) People under 14 are not allowed into bar areas of public houses.
   (iii) People under 18 are not allowed to buy alcohol or to drink at a bar.
   (iv) It is an offence to be drunk in a public place or to be drunk and disorderly.
   (v) It is an offence to drive under the influence of drink.
   (vi) Licensing laws restrict the times when alcohol may be sold.

(c) **Drugs**
Drugs are controlled in the main by two laws:

   (i) *The Medicines Act* which controls the manufacture and supply of medicines.

   (ii) *The Misuse of Drugs Act* which is designed to prevent harmful drugs being used for non-medical purposes. It is an offence to possess or supply drugs without legal authority and maximum sentences for breaking the law are severe.

It is also an offence to allow anyone on your premises to give or sell drugs to another person. Allowing the smoking of cannabis in your house is an offence.

TEST YOURSELF ON FACTS
True or False?
1. It is illegal to sell tobacco to anyone under 14.
2. People under 14 are not allowed into bar areas of public houses.
3. People under 16 are not allowed to buy alcohol.
4. People over 16 can drink non-alcoholic drinks in a public house.
5. Smoking a cigarette shortens life by five minutes.

---

2. MONEY MATTERS

(a) **Tobacco**
The tax on tobacco accounts for nearly three-quarters of the price of a packet of cigarettes. The gain to the Treasury is enormous and any Chancellor of the Exchequer would have a problem in replacing lost revenue if smoking were tightly controlled.

(b) **Alcohol**
£6000 million is paid to the Treasury from tax on drinks.
£200 million is spent on alcohol advertisements every year.

(c) **Drugs**
Obviously the government does not collect a tax on illegal drugs. The high prices go to the suppliers. In 1983/84 30–60 per cent pure heroin was being sold for £60–£80 per gram and an addict might use a quarter gram a day.

WHAT DO YOU THINK?
1. Is it morally right for the state to derive massive income from such harmful activities as smoking and drinking?
2. Should smoking be banned by law?

---

3. THE EXTENT OF THE PROBLEM

It is not the intention of this book to give you horrifying accounts of people who are dependent on tobacco, alcohol or drugs. You can read those in the newspapers and watch them on television. But you should know some facts.

(a) Tobacco

Forty per cent of the adult population are smokers yet it is said that on average each cigarette shortens the life of a regular smoker by five and a half minutes. Women who smoke during pregnancy are likely to have smaller babies and run a heightened risk of losing the baby. The connection between smoking and cancer is recognised. According to the DHSS, tobacco contributes to at least 100,000 premature deaths in the United Kingdom each year.

(b) Alcohol

Well over ninety per cent of the adult population drink to some extent. The consumption among those in their late teens and early twenties is 40–50 per cent above the average. Yet one-third of drivers and a quarter of all adult pedestrians killed in road accidents had blood levels over the legal limit. The Royal College of Physicians calculate that several hundred thousand people in Britain may be dependent on alcohol and 25,000 premature deaths each year are linked to alcohol abuse.

(c) Drugs

During 1983 over 10,200 heroin addicts were known to the Home Office. The total number of regular users is likely to be as high as 50,000. Look again at the price they are likely to have to pay for the drug. The connection between drugs and crime is then surely easily made.

CHRISTIAN PERSPECTIVES

The Church is often accused of being against pleasures which people enjoy. Yet the psalmist praises God for 'wine that maketh glad the heart of man' (Ps. 104.15), wine is used at Holy Communion and it seems that Jesus himself was criticised for being a drinker (Luke 7.34).

> ### SUGGESTIONS FOR BIBLE STUDY
> **Proverbs 23.29–32**
> **Romans 13.13–14**

The key to a Christian understanding of the problem is to be found by looking at whether or not the individual is in control of the situation. For some people **temperance** (= moderate drinking) is impossible. If that is the case being a **teetotaller** (= not drinking alcohol at all) is the only sensible alternative. Similarly with drugs. They are not evil in themselves; they can be a great blessing. It is their misuse which is wrong. Christians believe that people have a responsibility for the use they make of God's gifts. Chief among these gifts is the body in which we live. Destroying that makes a person no use to God or his fellow human beings.

Christians also believe that the money they possess is to be used for God's work. Looking after themselves is part of that work but anyone would find it difficult to make out a case for spending large sums of money on misusing drugs.

> ### CHECK YOUR UNDERSTANDING
> 1. What does 'temperance' mean?
> 2. What is a teetotaller?
> 3. Write a paragraph explaining the Christian view on addiction.

Some Christians, notably the Salvation Army, who have wide experience of working with addicts, make it a rule never to touch alcohol themselves. Some Christian denominations use unfermented grape juice rather than wine at Holy Communion. These are views which can be respected but they are not rules for all Christians.

The attitude of the Church can be summed up as 'hating the sin but loving the sinner'. Christians are active in social work among addicts of all kinds. In serving the person in need, they believe they are serving Christ himself (look again at the parable of the sheep and the goats from Matt. 25.31–45).

At the same time they take active steps to prevent harm wherever possible. The 'Parrot and Palm Cocktail Club' in Worthing is a case in point. It caters for 14–24 year olds by providing soft drinks in congenial, sophisticated surroundings. It is a successful and profitable place and obviously meets a need.

> ### COURSEWORK
> Write a play about someone addicted to *either* smoking *or* alcohol. Make a list of all the people affected by the addiction (there are likely to be more than you at first think) and make sure you write parts for them all. Work out how the addict is to be helped. Try out the play on the class to make sure it works, make any necessary changes and then submit the script as part of your coursework.

UNIT 16 | Mental Illness & Mental Handicap

TO START YOU TALKING

1. Any mother's first question is likely to be 'Is my baby all right?' How do you think you would react if you were told that your child was handicapped?
2. Should handicapped people be cared for in special hospitals or in the community?

INFORMATION

Make quite sure that you understand the difference between mental illness and mental handicap. *Anyone*, of any level of intelligence, may become mentally ill. People recover from mental illness but mental handicap means that, for all sorts of medical reasons which need not concern you here, the individual is born with a crippled brain which cannot develop beyond an elementary level. Such people have difficulty in learning the simplest things and recovery is not possible. All these conditions which may be acutely distressing for the victims also place a considerable burden on their families.

1. MENTAL ILLNESS

Mental illness is not a joke; nor is it a disgrace. It cannot be caught but just develops.

(a) Types of mental illness

The symptoms of some mental illnesses are more severe forms of states known to us all. Phobias, for example, are excessive fears; claustrophobia is terror in confined spaces; agoraphobia is fear of open spaces. A person suffering from agoraphobia may be unable to face leaving the house and is powerless to do anything about it. Other mental illnesses cut people off from friends and family since the patient is no longer able to relate to other people. Illnesses of this kind include autism and schizophrenia. Some mental illnesses such as senile dementia (= confusion) are related to the ageing process. Depressive illnesses recur in individuals and their 'blackness' is terrifying while it lasts.

(b) Statistics

In an interview with Stuart Sutherland in *The Times*, 16 July 1987, it was stated that one woman in six and one man in nine will spend some period of her or his life in a psychiatric hospital so it is very likely that yourself will either be admitted or will visit a friend or relative in a psychiatric hospital during your lifetime. In addition to people who are actually admitted to hospital, one person in four experiences mental distress in

some form. Think how many members of your own family cannot sleep without sleeping tablets, need to take tranquillisers or smoke or drink to relieve stress.

Half the patients admitted to psychiatric hospitals are discharged within a month and ninety per cent in less than a year. Half the total number of hospital beds in the country are occupied by people suffering from mental problems.

(c) The Law

The 1959 Mental Health Act allows compulsory admission if the patient is likely to be a danger to himself or others. The patient may then be detained for up to seventy-two hours while a decision is made as to whether the crisis has passed or whether long-term treatment is needed.

The majority of patients, however, enter hospital voluntarily.

TEST YOURSELF ON FACTS
1. What are phobias?
2. What proportion of (a) men, (b) women, will spend some period of their lives in a psychiatric hospital?
3. What proportion of hospital beds is occupied by patients suffering from mental problems?
4. What is the main provision of the 1959 Mental Health Act?

2. MENTAL HANDICAP

The mental handicap which is perhaps best known because it is easy to recognise is Down's Syndrome. It is caused at the time of conception. Each human cell has twenty-three pairs of chromosomes; one extra chromosome in each cell produces the symptoms of Down's Syndrome. It does not usually run in families but the risk of having such a child increases with the age of the mother. Not all mentally handicapped people look unusual; many look the same as everyone else.

Parents who are faced with the news that their child is mentally handicapped are likely to be put in touch with MENCAP (Royal Society for Mentally Handicapped Children and Adults) who have wide experience to offer. For example parents with a Down's Syndrome baby can be put in touch with the Down's Children's Association (DCA) and will be able to meet other parents who have been through the same experience.

Parents often feel resentment that such a thing should have happened to them and then feel guilty about their resentment. They know that, when they die, the 'child' is likely to have to go into an institution and friends and relatives, seeing the tensions caused by the child, may press them to 'put the child away now'. Other children in the family may well resent the extra attention which the handicapped child has to receive. Some families rise heroically to the challenge but those who sink under the burden need to be helped not despised.

CHECK YOUR UNDERSTANDING

1. What is the difference between mental illness and mental handicap?
2. Name three problems likely to be faced by the families of mentally handicapped children.

It is quite possible for most mentally handicapped people to be trained to look after themselves and even to be employed in simple routine work. For example one workshop employs them in folding maps. Each person learns to make one fold and passes the map on to the next until the job is complete.

Such a level of independent life is only possible where there is understanding and sympathy from the general public. One training centre had worked hard to train its mentally handicapped employees to be able to make a bus journey on their own, coping with buying a ticket to take them to work. The training was undone by the thoughtlessness of some schoolchildren on the bus who jeered at the handicapped making them too frightened to attempt the journey again.

CHRISTIAN PERSPECTIVES

SUGGESTIONS FOR BIBLE STUDY

Luke 10.25–37	Matt. 6.9
Gal. 5.22	Mark 3.31–35

Many people shy away from the difficulties of mental illness and mental handicap, but read the parable of the Good Samaritan (Luke 10.25–37).

(i) What did the good Samaritan do for the injured man? (*Be precise*).
(ii) What did Jesus say at the end to the man who had asked 'Who is my neighbour?'
(iii) Which of the fruits of the Holy Spirit listed by St Paul in Gal. 5.22 could be shown towards people suffering from mental disorders?
(iv) How did Jesus tell his followers to address God in Matt. 6.9?
(v) Who does Jesus say is his brother/sister in Mark 3.31–35?

Write a summary of what these biblical insights tell of the Christian attitude to mental illness and mental handicap.

WHAT DO YOU THINK?

1. Discuss the advantages and disadvantages of caring for the mentally ill and the mentally handicapped within the community. What difficulties can you foresee? How can these be overcome?
2. Should the mentally handicapped be sterilised? You need to consider their need for love, their inability to understand the consequences of their actions, the future of any children born to them and, on the other hand, the sanctity of life. Does anyone have the right to make such a decision? If so, who?

COURSEWORK

Everyone needs a sense of belonging. How can this be achieved for (i) the mentally handicapped, (ii) families who feel isolated by the pressures of caring for a mentally handicapped child? What can you yourself do to ease the isolation of families in this situation?

Consult local professional workers and voluntary groups in the field about their experience. Decide how much time you can give on a regular basis and prepare a programme of action. Then put it into practice!

You will then be in a position to write at length on the needs of the mentally handicapped in the community.

TO START YOU TALKING

Check your own prejudices. What is your idea of the following?

(a) A duchess, a doctor, a shop assistant, a carpenter, a dustman.
(b) A secretary, a train driver, a nurse, a vicar, a stockbroker.
(c) A Jew, a Sikh, a Buddhist, a Roman Catholic, a Pentecostalist.
(d) A Scotsman, a Frenchman, a Jamaican, a Norwegian, a Japanese.

INFORMATION

1. PREJUDICE

It is very probable that the above exercise has produced a kind of cartoon version of the groups in question (= **stereotyping**) – harmless enough unless your knowledge of them never grows beyond that first prejudiced picture.

Prejudice is a matter of *pre-judging* people, allowing emotion to take over without factual basis. When this happens, particularly if you come to believe in your stereotyped picture, you are breaking the Golden Rule. (If you have forgotten what that is, check in Matt. 7.12). The groups you considered above cover the four main areas of prejudice – class, sex, religion, race. We shall look at each in turn.

2. CLASS PREJUDICE

British society is still riddled with class prejudice although there are signs of gradual improvement. Another word for this is snobbery, i.e. looking down on somebody from a sense of false superiority or valuing a person according to things which have nothing to do with a person's worth as a human being.

Here are some of the ways in which class distinctions are identified:

(a) Occupation

A doctor enjoys a status above that of a dustman although the work of both is vital for society. To some extent status is derived from the educational standards required for a professional qualification but some prestige also comes from associating with similarly favoured social contacts.

When a market research interviewer stops you in the street to find out your opinions, the interview is likely to include a question about your occupation through which you will be placed in one of the Registrar General's five classifications of social class. These are:

(i) Professional
(ii) Managerial and technical
(iii) Skilled manual/white collar workers
(iv) Semi-skilled manual workers
(v) Unskilled manual workers

These classifications provide a clue to life-style which is valuable in market research.

(b) Income

Social status does not come from level of income alone. A pop singer may well earn more than the prime minister but this does not confer superior class status. Even the rich are divided into those who have made their money and those who have inherited it. 'Old money' sometimes despises the newly rich. People descended from the former land-owning aristocracy still tend to marry within a narrow range of families so that money and status are preserved.

(c) Education

This is a decisive factor in sorting out the various levels of the middle class since educational achievement is likely to decide whether or not managerial status is reached.

TEST YOURSELF ON FACTS
1. What are the four main areas of prejudice?
2. What are the Registrar General's five classifications of social class?
3. What is the meaning of 'snobbery'?

Social class attitudes show themselves in a variety of ways. Notice your own class attitudes in the following situations:

(i) *Accent*
Do you tease people at school who speak with a

'posh' accent? Why? Why should some regional dialects be more acceptable socially than others? Can you name some of these?

(ii) *Attitude to child training*
Work out for yourselves how you would expect children from the Registrar General's classes 1 and 5, who are still young enough to be under their parents' control, to spend their leisure time. Do these activities reflect different parental expectations for them?

(iii) *Leisure pursuits*
Is there a social class difference between rugger and soccer crowds? What about lacrosse? darts? snooker? polo? Which social classes enjoy these sports?

(iv) *Listening and viewing habits*
Is there a class difference between BBC1 and BBC2? What about Radio 1 and Radio 3?

(v) *Reading habits*
As long ago as 1964 a national survey investigating parental attitudes to school used as one of its criteria the number of books found in the home. Two-thirds of unskilled workers' homes had five books or fewer.

You can become aware of your own prejudices by noticing honestly the extent to which you would be aware of any of these factors and how far they would influence you in forming an opinion of a person's worth.

CHRISTIAN PERSPECTIVES

SUGGESTIONS FOR BIBLE STUDY
James 2.1–6

1. Snobbery

Snobbery obviously existed in the early Church as can be seen from this extract from the letter of James.

Write out verses 4–6a in your own words.

CHECK YOUR UNDERSTANDING
Read the following poem and answer the questions.

> My parents kept me from children who were rough
> And who threw words like stones and who wore torn clothes.
> Their thighs showed through rags. They ran in the street
> And climbed cliffs and stripped by the country streams.
>
> I feared more than tigers their muscles like iron
> And their jerking hands and their knees tight on my arms
> I feared the salt coarse pointing of those boys
> Who copied my lisp behind me on the road.
>
> They were lithe, they sprang out behind hedges
> Like dogs to bark at our world. They threw mud
> And I looked another way, pretending to smile.
> And I longed to forgive them, yet they never smiled.
> (*Stephen Spender from Collected Poems*)

(i) What is it about the boy in the poem which the other children dislike?
(ii) How do they show their dislike?
(iii) What is the 'our world' referred to in the third verse?
(iv) How does the boy react to the bullying?
(v) How can such barriers be broken down?

2. Brotherhood

The Christian understanding of the fatherhood of God leads to the realisation that every human being is brother or sister and, according to Christian belief, a person for whom Christ died. There is therefore no room for class prejudice.

COURSEWORK

Take any work of English literature (your English teacher will help you choose) and analyse the social class attitudes shown in it. You may well be able to combine this work with your English studies.

TO START YOU TALKING

Should a woman sacrifice her own career for the sake of her family?

INFORMATION

1. THE LAW

Under the Sex Discrimination Act 1975 it is unlawful to discriminate in recruitment, promotion or training on grounds of sex. This applies to men as well as to women as was made clear when men faced opposition to their training in midwifery. Job advertisements must not discriminate on grounds of sex, although they may succeed in discouraging applicants of both sexes from applying through their wording. For example it is possible to say that applicants for teaching posts should be prepared to help with boys' games. Nevertheless, if applicants of both sexes still apply, they must be treated equally. There are still exceptions. By law women may not work underground, nor does the law force the Church to accept women for ordination to the priesthood. Many would regard a male priesthood as a case of sex being a 'Genuine Occupational Qualification (GOQ), which is recognised in the Act.

TEST YOURSELF ON FACTS

1. What is the main provision of the 1975 Sex Discrimination Act?
2. Give three reasons for sexual prejudice.
3. List three problems met by mothers returning to work.

---

2. REASONS FOR PREJUDICE

A woman's working life is affected by her biological function of motherhood and most of the prejudices she meets in the field of employment stem from this fact, i.e.

(a) Women are likely to take a break from full-time employment for child-bearing. If they do not return to work immediately it is possible they will experience difficulty because:
   (i) They themselves lose confidence.
   (ii) Their skills become rusty.
   (iii) Their knowledge and experience become out of date.

(b) Employers fear absenteeism in a mother when she experiences the conflicting demands of job and family.
(c) Sexual stereotyping still exists in some areas of employment. (*Can you think of jobs where girls might still find it hard to succeed?*)

CHRISTIAN PERSPECTIVES

1. THE ORDINATION OF WOMEN

The Church is deeply divided over the issue of whether women can be priests. Many Free Churches have women as ministers but Roman Catholic and Orthodox Christians reject women as priests. The Church of England is undecided and divided. Anglicans in, for example, Canada, the United States of America and New Zealand have ordained women as priests but these women may not function as priests in countries which have not accepted women in this role. The issue came to a head in 1989 when Anglicans in the United States chose a woman bishop and the Pope wrote to the Archbishop of Canterbury to point out that women priests presented a stumbling block to greater unity between the Anglican Church and Roman Catholics.

Copy the following statements into your books and beside each draw four boxes marked 'Strongly agree', 'Agree', 'Disagree', 'Strongly disagree'. Tick the appropriate box.

(a) The Church is not free to change the pattern set by Jesus who chose twelve men to be his apostles.
(b) The priest represents the *whole* people of God, male and female. There is therefore no reason why women should not become priests.
(c) No single branch of the Church should act on its own in a matter as basic as the nature of priesthood.
(d) When he is celebrating Holy Communion the priest represents Christ himself and it disturbs profound imagery if women play this particular role.
(e) As women can do anything else in the modern world, there is no reason why they should not do this as well.
(f) In the New Testament the Church is described as 'the bride of Christ'. Receiving him, they become fruitful. The imagery is sexual but the issue is not a matter of sexual prejudice.

CHECK YOUR UNDERSTANDING

1. Write an essay explaining both sides of the debate over the ordination of women and state your own opinion at the end.
2. It has been shown that girls achieve better results in maths and science in single-sex schools. Can you suggest why this should be so? Would it be true in your own school?

SUGGESTIONS FOR BIBLE STUDY
1 Corinth. 11.11–12
Eph. 5.22–30

2. ST PAUL

St Paul is sometimes held up as an example of male chauvinism at its most tiresome. It is necessary to read him in as unprejudiced a way as possible taking into account his own life and times. His own environment influenced him in a number of ways:

(a) Paul believed the end of the world to be imminent and therefore the most important thing required of a Christian was whole-hearted devotion to God. Whether a person was married or not was of little importance when the end was expected soon.

(b) Paul himself was celibate and so perhaps inclined to recommend the state which served him well.
(c) Some of his pronouncements were made in the context of a particular problem in a particular Christian community.

Now read what he has to say in the passages suggested in the box.

What does he say about the relationship between men and women in 1 Corinth. 11.11–12?

How, according to Eph. 5.25 are men to love their wives?

(Remember that Christ died for the Church.) Do the marriage vows (p. 15) reflect this pronouncement?

WHAT DO YOU THINK?
As St Paul was writing for people living in an environment very different from our own, is anything to be gained from studying what he has to say about relationships?

COURSEWORK
A Radio Interview
Find a woman working in a traditionally man's world and a man working in a traditionally female environment. Perhaps there are former pupils of your school in these positions. Interview them (not necessarily together), preferably using a tape recorder, to find out

(a) What made them choose their work.
(b) What prejudices they had to meet in their training in their work.
(c) Any practical difficulties they have to overcome in their work.
(d) Any prejudices they meet from clients.
(e) Whether they would recommend others to follow in their footsteps.

TO START YOU TALKING

1. **Brainstorming**
   In precisely two minutes list areas of conflict in the world where religion is involved.
2. Now discuss why religion causes conflict.
3. Is one justified in attempting to convert adherents of other faiths to one's own?

INFORMATION

It is beyond the scope of this book to examine the beliefs of the world's religions and the prejudices to which they give rise but we can look at a few of the religious beliefs and practices which you are likely to meet at school or at work and at what needs to be done to accommodate them. Religious intolerance arises either from a desire to make others conform to one's own way of thinking or from ignorance of the importance of certain practices to believers.

1. PRAYER AND FESTIVALS

Our society is organised around Christian festivals. Whether Christian or not everyone has a holiday at Christmas and Easter and the weekend gives Sundays free. Jews have different festivals but their Sabbath comes within the weekend. For Muslims, however, Friday is a day of compulsory communal midday prayer (*Jumua*) and they must pray five times each day. Although there is some flexibility, at least two of these prayer times come during normal working hours.

Before praying Muslims must ritually wash in clear running water and they need 15–30 minutes in all for this prayer time. Where Muslims are employed tolerance of this practice is needed. Usually a flexible lunch break and the provision of a quiet room is sufficient but other employees have been known to complain that such flexibility is unfair.

It is the same with festivals. Some workers use up days of holiday to accommodate them but this may not always be necessary. For example, during the month of Ramadan Muslims must fast from sunrise till sunset. The great festival of Id al Fitr comes at the end. It should not be beyond the ability of employers to allow Muslims to work through their meal breaks during Ramadan and so build up entitlement to time off at the end for Id al Fitr.

2. DIET

Canteens used by the adherents of different faiths need to provide for their needs. For example Hindus are

vegetarians. This is in accordance with their doctrine of *ahimsa* (= reverence for life). Many are strict to the point of not eating eggs or fish. Milk, yoghurt and butter are acceptable since no killing is involved in producing them. Hindus do not drink alcohol. Sikhs, although not quite such strict vegetarians, follow a similar diet.

Jews should only eat *kosher* food which fulfils certain regulations found in their law and some foods are totally forbidden, e.g. pork products.

Muslims may not eat pork. Other meat must be slaughtered in a particular way (*halal*). They do not drink alcohol. From time to time animal rights organisations question the legality of the ritual slaughter required by *halal* or *kosher* regulations fearing that an unacceptable level of suffering is caused. Before making up your own minds, wait until you have studied factory farming methods (Unit 34). You may then question the public's right to criticise.

3. CLOTHING

The 'five Ks' of the Sikh religion have caused problems with employers, i.e.

Keshas	(= uncut hair)
Kangha	(= comb worn under the turban)
Kachha	(= shorts)
Kara	(= steel bracelet)
Ghatra Kirpan	(= small sword)

Women wear trousers and often a headscarf to cover their hair. Problems arise with employers in three main areas — safety, hygiene regulations and uniforms. Do you think it reasonable to debar Sikhs from applying for jobs where such difficulties may arise or should we, in a multi-cultural society be prepared to tolerate variations on religious grounds?

CHRISTIAN PERSPECTIVES

SUGGESTIONS FOR BIBLE STUDY
Romans 14

Within the framework of Christianity prejudice still exists between Catholics and Protestants. Find out for yourselves what really goes on in churches of both kinds. The buildings themselves express something of the convictions of the people who worship in them.

1. THINGS TO LOOK FOR IN A CATHOLIC CHURCH

(a) **The font**

This is usually found near the door as a reminder that individuals become Christians ('enter the Church') through baptism. You may see people dipping fingers into the water and signing themselves with a cross. This is to remind themselves of their baptism.

(b) The altar

This is the focal point since it is here that Catholics believe that Christ comes to them in the Mass. It will probably have beautiful hangings the colour of which is changed according to the Church's seasons.

(c) Statues with candles alight near them

Catholics do not worship the Virgin Mary. Worship belongs to God alone. They honour her as the human being who made possible the incarnation by saying 'Yes' to God. Catholics ask saints, who they believe to be their brothers and sisters in Christ, to join their prayers with their own and they light a candle as a sign of prayer.

(d) Confessionals

The prejudiced view is that Catholics can confess their sins and blithely go out and repeat them. The informed person knows that repentance is the first requirement of someone going to Confession and a firm intention not to sin again is the second.

St John's Parish Church, Sevenoaks, Kent.

Wellington Square Baptist Church, Hastings.

2. THINGS TO NOTICE IN A PROTESTANT CHURCH

(a) Plainness

Nothing must be allowed to distract the worshipper from God.

(b) The pulpit

This will be in a prominent position emphasising the importance of preaching the gospel and the importance of the Bible. Protestant faith is grounded in the Bible and Christian doctrines not found there are rejected.

(c) Ten commandments

These may well be set out in a prominent position.

CHECK YOUR UNDERSTANDING

1. Why is the font traditionally near the door?
2. Why is the altar the focal point in a Catholic church?
3. Why is the pulpit prominent in Protestant churches?
4. Explain the importance of the Virgin Mary to Catholics.
5. What is the significance of candles in Catholic churches?

COURSEWORK

Visit a Catholic *and* a Protestant church, if possible for a service. Ask about anything you do not understand and then write an account of the way in which both the building itself and the form of worship express the beliefs of that particular group of Christians.

TO START YOU TALKING

Imagine that you have gone to work in China (if you are familiar with Chinese life choose a different country). How would you feel? Excited? Nervous? Would it make any difference to your feelings if you had been forced out of your own country? How much of your national life would you wish to retain? Would you wish to become identified with China? Would you eat Chinese food at home? Assuming you manage to learn Chinese, would you speak it together at home? Would you want your children to be brought up as Chinese? Would you retain your own religion? How would you expect Chinese people to treat you? Would you hope/expect to marry a Chinese? Would you expect opposition from your family?

INFORMATION

In this Unit the word 'black' is used to describe all ethnic minorities who suffer from the experience of racism whatever the colour of their skin.

(A) BRITAIN

Britain is a multi-racial society. This enriches our national life but only if two conditions are fulfilled. They are:

(a) Equality before the law which includes political equality.
(b) Equality of opportunity in employment, housing, education.

Where these conditions are not present **racism** exists.

In Britain today many laws are racist because they treat black people as the problem rather than tackling the problem of the attitudes of white people to their black neighbours.

Do you think racial prejudice can be changed by law?

1. Reasons for Racial Prejudice

Read the following remarks and work out the underlying cause of the racial prejudice:

(a) 'They're foreigners and you can't trust them.'
(b) 'The street doesn't seem the same since they arrived.'
(c) 'I've worked hard to get where I am. Why should they push in?'
(d) 'They say people are being laid off at the factory. Whose turn will it be next? Not the whites I hope.'
(e) 'You should smell their cooking! – puts you off your own.'
(f) 'Never even answered when I spoke to her. Looked proper scared.'
(g) 'Why should he be manager? Tom's white.'

2. Statistics

There are approximately 2.2 million black people in Britain, forty per cent of whom were born here. They form 4.3 per cent of the total population. Just over half are Asian and a quarter come from the Caribbean.

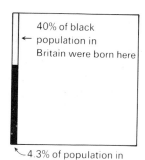

← 40% of black population in Britain were born here

↖ 4.3% of population in Britain are black people

They are concentrated in areas where the first arrivals found it easy to find work. Many of these areas now have unemployment problems. A survey by the Commission for Racial Equality in 1986 showed that unemployment among young black people was as high as 33 per cent compared with a rate for all ages and ethnic groups of 11 per cent.

3. The Law

There are two groups of racial laws:

(a) **Immigration laws**
These laws control who may enter Britain.

1948 *British Nationality Act* gave United Kingdom citizenship to anyone born in a British colony. At the time extra workers were needed particularly in the National Health Service. Since then more and more restrictions have been imposed.

1968 *Commonwealth Immigrants Act* allowed entry to British passport holders only if they were born, adopted, registered or naturalised British citizens or had a parent in one of those categories. This law kept out East African Asians who were suffering in Kenya and Uganda and who wanted a refuge in Britain.

The European Commission of Human Rights declared such racial discrimination to be degrading and a breach of the European Convention of Human Rights.

1981 *British Nationality Act.* This Act created three classes of citizenship:
  (i) British citizens
  (ii) British Dependent Territories Citizens (= those with a connection through a colony.)
  (iii) British Overseas Citizens who now need a voucher to settle in Britain. Obtaining a voucher takes about eight years.

A survey carried out by the Commission for Racial Equality in 1985 found that these laws were being used to enforce controls rather than to show concern for the rights of immigrants.

(b) Race Relations Laws

These laws are concerned with the treatment of ethnic minorities in Britain.

1968 *Race Relations Act* made it unlawful to treat one person less favourably than another on grounds of colour, race or ethnic origin in employment, trade unions, housing or in the provision of services offered to the public (e.g. hotels, shops, etc.). This Act did not work and its provisions were expanded in the
1976 *Race Relations Act* which also set up the Commission for Racial Equality to help people who suffer from discrimination.

TEST YOURSELF ON FACTS

1. Give four reasons for racial prejudice.
2. Approximately how many black people are there in Britain today?
3. What percentage were born here? What percentage of the population do they represent?
4. Name the three kinds of British Citizenship created in 1981.
5. What are the main provisions of the Race Relations Acts?

---

4. Evidence of Racial Discrimination

(a) Employment

In the 1940s and 1950s the majority of black citizens from the Commonwealth took semi-skilled or unskilled jobs. Forty years later, when more than forty per cent of black residents have been born and educated in Britain, that pattern has not changed.
Do you think this is a case of class or racial prejudice?

(b) Housing

Black people meet discrimination in housing. An investigation by the Greater London Council in a borough in the East End of London found that housing department staff were prejudiced against black people and that pressure from white tenants led to black people having poorer accommodation. Immigrant men cannot go on to housing lists until their families have arrived in Britain, which can take years to arrange, so new arrivals find themselves 'homeless' and in the worst possible temporary accommodation.

(c) Social Services

It is only comparatively recently that DHSS leaflets have been translated into minority languages. It follows that black citizens are *less* likely than white to use the welfare services since they are unaware of many of their rights and fear racist attitudes in some staff. Furthermore immigrants arriving since 1971 are only allowed to bring dependants on condition that they do not use public funds, which includes Income Support.

(d) Education

In 1985 the Swann Committee produced a report on the education of ethnic minorities entitled *Education for All.* They found that black children suffered from racism and that teachers were unaware of their own racist attitudes. As a result black pupils were being set at levels below their ability. The Swann Committee said it was a racist practice to provide separate classes in English as a second language since such classes result in children missing lessons in other subjects and so falling behind.

Few black children go on to train as teachers. The influence of black teachers would help the fight against racist attitudes.

Would it be better for people with special learning needs to be educated in separate schools? Think VERY carefully. Can you foresee dangers? What alternatives can you suggest?

CHECK YOUR UNDERSTANDING

1. What conditions lead to racism?
2. How did the 1968 Commonwealth Immigrants Act break the European Convention of Human Rights?
3. Why do comparatively few black people use Social Services?
4. Why did the Swann Committee regard lessons in English as a second language in schools as racist?
5. What is the difference between apartheid and colour prejudice?

(B) SOUTH AFRICA

1. Apartheid

The South African government believes that the only way in which white and coloured races can co-exist is through 'separate development'. So they practise racial segregation (= apartheid) but, following President de Klerk's release of Nelson Mandela from prison in 1990, change is in the air in South Africa.

If races develop separately, what are the likely results in politics, employment, housing and the law? Watch for news items from South Africa to help you work it out for yourselves.

2. The Law

Non-whites have to carry a pass. People may be arrested and imprisoned for ninety days without trial. Until 1985 white and non-white people could not mix let alone marry. Even now couples of mixed race need a permit to live together and must live in the area of the darker partner. Their children are classified as 'coloured' (= people of mixed race). **Banning orders** can be imposed. The effect of these is to put the individual virtually under house arrest. The person concerned is not allowed to meet more than one person at a time, so it is not possible even to go to church. They may not take part in any political activity nor may they be quoted in the press. Unrest against these laws has grown steadily over the past quarter century.

In 1982 a new Internal Security Act gave police powers to arrest people and to hold them indefinitely without trial and without access to outsiders if they were thought to be a threat to security.

CHRISTIAN PERSPECTIVES

Jesus himself was from the Middle East and, in terms of current race legislation, was black. He would have found it difficult to settle in modern Britain. This is a sobering thought for Christians.

SUGGESTIONS FOR BIBLE STUDY	
Lev. 19.33–34	Gal. 3.26–28
Ruth	Matt. 25.31–45

1. The Jewish laws set out in the Old Testament took care of aliens. Copy the two verses from Lev. 19.33–34 into your books and decorate them appropriately.

2. The Book of Ruth was written to bring home the fact that King David, the greatest of the Jewish kings, was descended from a mixed marriage. Read Ch. 2. How did Boaz treat the foreigner, Ruth? Say in detail.

3. On what grounds does St Paul say that the whole human race belongs to one family? (Gal. 3.26–28).

4. Look again at the parable of the sheep and the goats in Matt. 25.31–45. According to the parable, who is suffering when strangers are rejected?

5. A statement from the World Council of Churches in 1980 said 'Every human being created in the image of God is a person for whom Christ died. Racism, which is the use of a person's racial origin to determine a person's value, is an assault on Christ's values, and a rejection of his sacrifice.'

6. *World Council of Churches' Programme to Combat Racism*
This has been a controversial plan. A fund was created to provide help to organisations which supported victims of racial injustice. Some of the money inevitably went to revolutionary organisations such as the Patriotic Front in Zimbabwe even though the grants themselves were for spending on basic needs such as food and health care. The Church was accused of encouraging guerilla fighters and some churches withdrew from the WCC. Neither the Church of England nor Christian Aid gives money to this particular fund.

COURSEWORK

1. Prepare a report on the attitude of sportsmen and women towards participating in games in South Africa. Study specific examples of controversy and make your own views clear.

2. Carry out an investigation of your own school's record of racial awareness, e.g. Is History taught from the point of view of white people? In English, have you considered books, plays or films which explore racial issues? Is it possible for pupils from other countries to take public examinations in their heritage languages? How many black teachers do you have on the staff? What is your education teaching you to prepare you for life in a multi-racial society? What are the racial attitudes of pupils and staff?

Martin Luther King

(1929–1968)

Have you ever come under the spell of a great orator? Perhaps such people only emerge in times of crisis. In the fifties and sixties America produced such an orator in Martin Luther King, a negro and great leader, who inspired black Americans and gave them courage at a difficult time in their history.

There were 22 million black Americans at the time but without equal rights of citizenship with white Americans. Martin Luther King himself went to an all-Negro primary school in Atlanta, where he had been born in 1929. He could remember seeing members of the Ku Klux Klan, a white terrorist organisation, attacking negroes in the streets and was only six years old when he discovered that white parents would not allow their children to play with him.

He became famous at the age of 26. It happened because of a boycott of buses in Montgomery, Alabama, where he was pastor of a local church. Mrs Rosa Parks, a black seamstress in a large store, was returning home from work when a white passenger boarded the full bus. The law required a black person to give up a seat if the bus were full but Mrs Parks was tired, sat tight and politely refused to move. Police were called and she was arrested.

From that incident sprang the Montgomery bus boycott which lasted for 382 days and changed the life of the black community. For over a year black people refused to use the buses. It was a costly sacrifice but they brought the bus company to the point of bankruptcy and, more important, the US Supreme Court intervened declaring segregation to be illegal. Notice that the change was brought about by *non-violent* means.

In the southern states, where segregation had been practised for so long, change could not be brought about overnight. The next dramatic move occurred in September 1957 at Little Rock Arkansas. Although schools had been officially desegregated, the state governor used troops to bar nine negro children from attending a white school. The US President sent Federal troops to escort the children, and at last American citizens awoke to what was happening in their midst.

By now a Civil Rights organisation had been formed called the Southern Christian Leadership Conference. They planned campaigns in one city after another moving in to highlight particular problems; for example sitting-in in 'Whites only' restaurants, riding on 'Whites only' buses (these became known as 'Freedom riders') and crowding into 'Whites only' parks. In many places white Americans reacted violently but, such were the leadership qualities of Martin Luther King, black people behaved with dignified restraint. News pictures highlighted the contrast between the behaviour of blacks and whites to the detriment of the whites.

In the early 1960s John Kennedy was running for president. It was a close-run campaign and he needed the support of black voters. Martin Luther King seized the opportunity to win concessions for black people without having to resort to violence. He met the President in October 1962 and was able to press for action on Civil Rights issues. The next year he was joined by many white people in a great march in Washington to draw attention to a Civil Rights Bill being considered by Congress. At the Lincoln Memorial on this occasion he made one of his most famous speeches. 'I have a dream. It is a dream that is deeply rooted in the American dream. I have a dream that one day this nation will rise up, live out the true meaning of its creed: "We hold these truths to be self-evident, that all men are created equal." '

The Bill became law in 1964 but, by that time, President Kennedy had been assassinated and Martin Luther King fell foul of his successor through his opposition to the war in Vietnam. The Bill did not go as far as black people had hoped so the campaigning continued.

That year, at the age of 35, Martin Luther King became the youngest person ever to be awarded the Nobel Peace Prize. The 54,000 dollars prize money went into Civil Rights activities and the honour ensured maximum publicity for the cause.

His next campaign was designed to give negroes the vote. In Selma, Alabama, 15,000 black Americans were eligible to vote but, for a variety of petty reasons, only 333 were allowed to do so. Martin Luther King led marches of negroes to the court house to ask for the vote. As more and more of them were arrested he wrote from prison 'There are more negroes in jail with me than there are on the voting rolls.' From now on, whenever the Nobel Peace Prize winner was arrested or put in prison, it was news and provided adverse publicity for America throughout the world. Nevertheless police and troops violently harassed marching protesters. Supporters streamed in from other parts of America and King's non-violent upholding of the rights and human dignity of black people became an embarrassment to the government. At last the US President announced that he would give top priority to a Voting Rights Bill.

At the time of his assassination in 1968, Martin Luther King was on his way to support a march of dustmen. He had learned to live with threats not only to his own life but also to the lives of his family. Like Gandhi whose example of non-violence he followed, he was shot but, as with Mahatma Gandhi, the success of his cause was assured. Not all the problems have been solved but the attitude of white people has been changed. It is no longer acceptable in the United States to behave in a racist fashion.

Poverty

Make two collections of pictures from newspapers and magazines illustrating (a) riches, (b) poverty. KEEP THESE PICTURES. You can use them again later in Unit 32, but at this point notice:

1. Which are easier to find?

2. Roughly what proportion of the pictures illustrating poverty are concerned with conditions in this country?

3. What kinds of deprivation are shown?

INFORMATION

Thirty per cent of the population are caught up in a level of poverty which has been brought about by circumstances largely outside their control. Look again at your collection of pictures. Does it come as a surprise to you that as many as thirty per cent of the population of this country are living in poverty? Poverty makes itself felt in the following ways:

1. SHORTAGE OF MONEY

The level of income below which people become eligible for Income Support is known as the **poverty line**. Not everybody below that level receives benefit. Some are not eligible; some have savings which, whilst not making them wealthy, disqualify them from receiving support. Others, particularly the elderly, who still have painful memories of insensitively means-tested national assistance in the period 1918–1939, refuse to apply for what is their right.

In addition to those *below* the poverty line there are over twelve million people within the DHSS definition of *low income*, i.e. incomes not more than 140 per cent above Income Support level. A sizeable percentage of the population are therefore in financial straits. Increasingly we hear politicians speaking about 'two nations'.

They do not mean the prejudiced views northerners and southerners have of each other. It is a comment on the division between rich and poor. In 1976 the wealthiest fifth of the population took 44.4 per cent of the nation's total income and the poorest fifth only 0.8 per cent. By 1986 these figures had increased/decreased to 50.7 per cent and 0.3 per cent respectively, i.e. the rich had grown richer and the poor poorer.

2. HOUSING

The United Nations Declaration of Human Rights states 'everyone has a right to a standard of living adequate for the health and well-being of himself and of his family, including food, clothing, housing . . .'.

The poor have a *right* to a home but housing is expensive and the lowest income groups suffer most from the lack of suitable rented accommodation.

About twenty-five per cent of houses in Britain were built before 1919 but in the inner cities that proportion can be as high as sixty per cent. Inevitably there is a depressing air of decay about them. Following the bombing of the Second World War, councils built high-rise blocks of flats despite the fact that tenants would have much preferred terrace houses with a patch of garden, however small. Many of these tower blocks are vandalised and sometimes uninhabitable. Lifts get broken, long dark corridors are dangerous after dark, walls are covered with grafitti, litter abounds. Such accommodation has proved to be unsuitable for some of the most vulnerable members of society. These include pensioners living alone, single-parent families and black people.

Much of the problem of inner city poverty arises from unemployment, a subject we shall consider in greater detail in Unit 23, but it is important at this stage to make it clear that the poor have suffered most from our economic decline, that it is not their own fault and that they are powerless to help themselves.

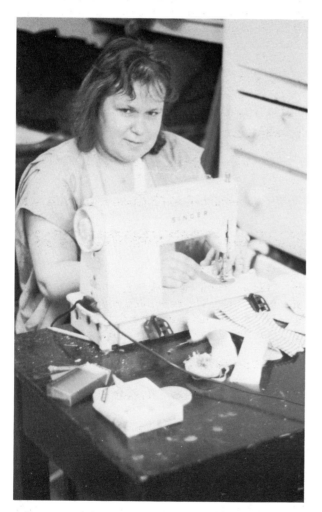

Young people in the Urban Area of Stockton-on-Tees have been helped to set up on their own in business through the Enterprise Training Centre, Stockton Anchorage.

3. RELATIONSHIPS

In a disintegrating society people find themselves lonely and friendless. The unemployed no longer come into daily contact with other people in their workplace.

Poverty leads to people becoming isolated. They can no longer afford to go out for an evening's entertainment and lack the money to invite friends home. Marriages are under strain with all that implies of stress for children. Yet these same people are confronted on all sides by the advertising of a materialistic society which urges them to buy more and more consumer goods.

Their inability to do so must increase their sense of deprivation, **alienation** (= sense of being cut off from society), inducing envy and so adding to the vicious circle of social disintegration.

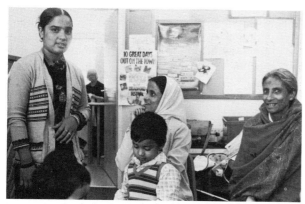

Local mums in a deprived inner-city area of Bradford get together to develop their skills and confidence at a Community Centre supported by the Church Urban Fund.

CHRISTIAN PERSPECTIVES

The Church is often told to keep out of politics – an issue to be considered in more detail in Unit 28 but, as the reasons for poverty are economic and political, a cure cannot be found by responding only at a personal level. That would be treating symptoms rather than the disease itself. Lotions may ease the itching of your spots but a doctor will want to treat whatever is causing them.

1. FAITH IN THE CITY

In 1985 an important report was published by the Archbishop of Canterbury's Commission on Urban Priority Areas. UPAs are areas of exceptional deprivation, mainly in our inner cities. The report is entitled *Faith in the City: a call for action by church and nation.* It was followed in 1988 by the launching of the *Church Urban Fund* to provide money for action in these areas. The Commission had investigated life in the inner cities of this country where some of the worst poverty is to be found and made recommendations for action. Repeatedly the report reminds us that statistics are about real people. We must not forget the individual, personal suffering which the figures represent. It says, *'Poverty is not only about shortage of money. It is about rights and relationships, about how people are treated and how they regard themselves; about powerlessness, exclusion and loss of dignity. Yet the lack of an adequate income is at its heart.'*

In 1990 a follow-up report, *Living Faith in the City,* found the situation unimproved and in some areas worse than before, although unemployment figures had fallen.

> ### SUGGESTIONS FOR BIBLE STUDY
> Deut. 15.7–11   Matt. 25.31–45
> Amos 5.7; 5.10–12   Luke 10.25–37   Gal. 6.2

2. OLD TESTAMENT

(a) **Deut. 15.7–11**
Jewish people had detailed laws which protected vulnerable members of society. What provision for the poor is made in this passage from Deuteronomy? What happened every seventh year?

God's chosen people were aware of a moral law beyond themselves and had developed their own practical form of 'social security'.

(b) **Amos 5.7 and 10–12**
The prophet Amos, in the eighth century BC saw a society just as polarised as our own and warned that injustice would not escape the judgement of God. For what reason does the prophet say the people are doomed?

Outwardly the people kept up an appearance of being religious but their lack of care for the poor condemned them. This judgement is not something imposed from outside. When a nation becomes selfish, grasping and uncaring, Society disintegrates and, in the case of Israel in the times of Amos, is incapable of withstanding attack by an enemy.

3. NEW TESTAMENT

(a) **Luke 10.25–37**
What insights into the treatment of poverty does the parable of the Good Samaritan offer?

(b) **Matt. 25.31–45**
According to the parable of the sheep and the goats, who is suffering in the poor?

(c) **Gal. 6.2**
What does St Paul tell Christians to do in Gal. 6.2?

> ### COURSEWORK
> Find out about the work of some of the following voluntary organisations which help people in deprived areas: Age Concern, Children's Society, Church Army, Community Service Volunteers, Dr Barnardo's, National Children's Homes, Salvation Army, Shelter, Simon Communities, Wel-care, Women's Aid.
> You will find their addresses in the notes at the end of this book. Be sure to enclose a stamp with any request for information.
>
> Then write at length about the part played by voluntary organisations in relieving the effects of poverty.

St Botolph's Crypt Centre

Can you imagine what it is like to be homeless? Perhaps you are a teenager who has been desperately unhappy at home and has come to the city to escape Perhaps you have been unemployed for months or even years and think you might find work in London. Perhaps you have been through a traumatic experience which you want to put behind you by pulling up roots and moving right away. There is no such thing as a 'typical case'. It demeans people to lump them together as 'the homeless' – or worse still as 'down and outs'. Each individual has the feelings, needs, hopes and fears common to us all. In 1981 the Department of the Environment published the results of a national survey called *Single and Homeless*. It showed how inaccurate are popular assumptions. Single homeless people are NOT drunken, disordered, inadequate vagrants. Another survey carried out by the GLC in 1985 showed that most people using a hostel in Tower Hamlets in East London had been in the area for some time – seventy-five per cent of them for four years or more. So their plight cannot be blamed on constantly moving from place to place.

Imagine you have arrived in London to look for work. You don't have much money but expect to find a job quite soon. You quickly find that without an address this is almost impossible. (*Why? Work it out for yourselves.*) So you look for cheap lodgings, but no landlord will take you in if you don't have a job. You're caught in the system. How long do you think you will stay clean and presentable for interviews if you are having to sleep rough? What happens if you get ill? Forty per cent of those using facilities for the homeless are not registered with a doctor. Many of them have been told that doctors' lists are full. Where can they look for help?

St Botolph's Crypt Centre in the City of London is one of a number of voluntary agencies trying to help people with no fixed abode. They offer useful facilities. Each evening from Monday to Thursday there is a 'drop in' session for two hours, with a social club on Friday nights.

Doors are open at 6.30 when everyone who comes is greeted individually. There is always a doctor and nurse on duty to help those in need of medical attention. Washing facilities and showers are available, and free soap, towels and razors are handed out to those who want them. There is a laundry room so that people can wash their clothes and get them dry. Free sandwiches and tea are provided. Above all there is somewhere to sit and be with friends in the warm. There may be a concert or a theatrical performance or it may just be an evening of companionship which puts fresh heart into those who come. At 8.30 they have to leave. In the depths of winter this is a bad moment for helpers and helped alike. There is no room for them to sleep in the crypt so they have to leave whatever the weather. Knowing that people will be sleeping rough, in squats or in one of the grim hostels which provide about a thousand beds per night in the City and East End of London brings home the enormity of the problem of the single homeless and induces a sense of powerlessness.

Some of you will be aware of the workings of Council Housing lists. When a person registers, his need is assessed according to a variety of factors for which points are awarded. When council accommodation becomes vacant it is allocated to those with the most points. Single people, even with no roof over their heads, are invariably at the bottom of the list. Knowing this, many of them don't even bother to register. Sales of council houses have reduced the number of homes available and safety

regulations have forced the closure of some of the older hostels. Unemployment brings more people to London in search of work. The problem seems insuperable.

Three days a week there is a Day Centre in the Crypt. People come for help in understanding the complexities of DHSS regulations; they come to talk about their problems or to seek help over finding somewhere to live. Nobody expresses a preference for sleeping rough. At midday everyone meets for a discussion which gives people the chance to talk about their feelings and sense of frustration with the system, and then comes lunch, when clients will be joined by any visitors. In the afternoons different kinds of activity are provided such as arts and crafts and drama and these help people to unwind and think and talk through their problems. There are no easy solutions. Voluntary agencies like St Botolph's can only ease the symptoms. A cure for the problem requires political action.

Meanwhile what can individuals do? Many schools support the work of St Botolph's through their Harvest Festivals. If you are too far away to be able to deliver tea, sugar and tinned food to the crypt, how about selling your harvest produce and sending them money instead? Staff at the Centre are involved in educational work, making people aware of the problems of homelessness. They visit schools and welcome small groups to the crypt. Why not write to the Administrator to find out? You will find the address at the back of this book. Remember to enclose at least a stamp.

TO START YOU TALKING

1. Put the following in the order you regard as most important in choosing a job:

   Good money from the start: good prospects: status: interest: the opportunity to serve other people: the opportunity to use your talents: short hours: training given on the job: congenial company: the feeling of doing something useful.

2. What are the differences between paid employment and the kind of work which a housewife or mother does at home? Looking at the list in the first question may provide you with some ideas. Is one of these kinds of work more satisfying or important than the other?

3. One of the first questions we ask a stranger when we are introduced is 'What do you do?' Why do we ask this? What does the answer convey to us about the person?

INFORMATION

1. PURPOSE OF WORK

The Victorians believed that if work were hard and unpleasant it was better for us and tended to value a person according to how hard he worked. This idea of hard work being a virtue is called the **Protestant work ethic**.

List the following purposes of work in the order you think most imortant:

(a) To provide food, clothing and shelter.
(b) To spend time in a constructive way.
(c) To contribute to the well-being of the community.
(d) To acquire self-respect.

TEST YOURSELF ON FACTS
1. What is meant by the Protestant work ethic?
2. Name three purposes of work.
3. What is meant by a 'vocation'?

---

2. REWARDS OF WORK

(a) **Money**
Why are some people paid much more than others? Is it a reflecton of the value society puts on their work?

(b) **Status**
Job descriptions use important-sounding names in the hope of appealing to the personal pride of the people doing them. Can you put these job titles into simpler terms? Administrative assistant: coiffeur: director of studies: horticultural consultant: rodent operator.

(c) **Satisfaction of using one's talents**
Society needs to make use of people's talents for the common good. Why are some people prevented from using their talents?

(d) **Fulfilling a vocation**
A vocation is a 'calling'. Some people feel they *must* do a certain job; there is a sense of fitness about their doing it. Usually the word is applied particularly to the caring professions such as nursing, teaching, the Church's ministry. Society is then apt to expect the individuals to find their satisfaction in the job rather than in their earnings. Is this attitude acceptable?

CHRISTIAN PERSPECTIVES

SUGGESTIONS FOR BIBLE STUDY
Gen. 2.15; 3.17–19   John 13.14–15
Prov. 6.6–11   2 Thess. 3.6–12
Matt. 20.1–16

---

1. PURPOSE OF WORK

(a) **Creation stories**
Christians believe that work is part of God's plan. The Creation stories show that work was ordained *before*

the Fall, i.e. it was not a punishment and, in Christian belief, only becomes burdensome when human beings act without considering God's will.

(b) Prov. 6.6–11

What are the lessons people could learn from studying ants?

(c) 2 Thess. 3.6–12

To understand the extract from St Paul's letter to the Thessalonians you need to know that news had reached him that some Christians, confident that the Second Coming was imminent, had stopped working and were sitting around waiting for it. Paul himself was a tent maker and, during his many journeyings, continued to earn his living by his trade. This is the situation to which he refers, i.e. one in which people have the opportunity to work but refuse, *not* one in which there is no work for them to do. What does St Paul say should happen to those who will not work?

WHAT DO YOU THINK?

Can you make out a case for everyone's being paid the same? What difficulties can you foresee? (Look again at Unit 8.)

---

2. REWARDS OF WORK

(a) Money

Read the parable of the workers in the vineyard (Matt. 20.1–16). It is one of the most controversial stories Jesus told. How would you have reacted if you had been working all day in the vineyard – be honest! Is the parable really about money? If not, what *is* it about? It is characteristic of the Christian attitude that money is *not* the main motivation for work (or anything else!)

(b) Status

Christians remember that Jesus washed the feet of his disciples (the work of a slave, i.e. a person with no status at all) and told them 'if I, your Lord and Master

have washed your feet, you also ought to wash one another's feet. I have set you an example: you are to do as I have done for you.' (John 13.14–15). Read the whole story (John 13.1–17). Service, not status, should therefore be the basic attitude of Christians to work.

(c) Satisfaction of using one's talents

The Christian view is that these are God-given and are to be used in his service. Because they have been *given* they should not be a source of pride. On the other hand Christians believe that false humility should be avoided. C. S. Lewis points out that there is something ridiculous about a pretty girl pretending she is plain or a clever one that she is a fool.

(d) Fulfilling a vocation

Christians believe that the sense of a 'calling' experienced by some people comes from God.

Do not think that because Christians speak in terms of service in applying Bible teaching to the subject of work that *only* the obviously caring professions are regarded as religiously suitable. This is not so. The grocer is serving his customers; the secretary serves her boss; the orchestral player is serving his audience and the composer; the computer operator is serving his employer; the bus driver is serving the community. Christians would regard all these as valid ways of obeying God and using one's talents.

CHECK YOUR UNDERSTANDING

1. *Explain Christian teaching about money, status, use of talents in relation to work.*
2. *Why would Christians think it wrong to regard work as a punishment?*
3. *Think of five jobs which Christians ought **not** to do. They are likely to be matters of individual conscience and not all Christians will reach the same conclusion about the same jobs.*

COURSEWORK

Write an essay about your own attitude to work explaining what you would look for in a job and what you would do with your time if you could not find work.

Explain the Christian teaching on the subject and say in what ways you agree/ disagree with it.

TO START YOU TALKING

Work in pairs

1. Would you be prepared to work fewer hours, even if take-home pay were not so high, in order for others to have some work?
2. Would you consider job sharing? i.e. two people covering one job at different times of the day. It is a pattern which suits many married women since it offers them greater flexibility. Could it be applied across a wider field?
3. Some older employees are content to take early retirement to make way for younger people who are unemployed. Would you be prepared to start work later − say at 18 instead of 16 − in order to reduce the numbers who have no work at all?

INFORMATION

(A) UNEMPLOYMENT

1. Statistics

In June 1989 6.4 per cent of the population of the United Kingdom were unemployed. Bearing in mind regional variations, the rate is considerably higher in some areas. More worrying, the proportion of the unemployed who had been out of work for more than three years had increased from 8 per cent in July 1983 to nearly 21.4 per cent in July 1989.

Find out the total number unemployed in the month in which you are studying this Unit. What total of the population does that represent?

2. Causes of Unemployment

Find out the main causes of unemployment in your own area. Make contact with a class in a school in a totally different kind of area and exchange information on this subject.

3. Effects of Unemployment

The effects of unemployment are measured in terms of human misery.

(a) Loss of self-respect

There is evidence that a person's self-image depends on what he does and the attitude of society to his work. When someone no longer has work self-respect is sharply diminished.

(b) Strain on marriages

The divorce rate among the unemployed is double the national average. Constant failure in the search for work leads to irritability and an increase in mental illness and this is bound to be reflected in unhappiness within the family.

(c) Increase in crime

Lord Scarman's inquiry into the causes of the Brixton riots noted that there had been a sharp increase in the number of burglaries which was directly attributable to unemployment in the area.

(d) 'Knock-on' effect

When people are unemployed obviously their spending power is diminished and small corner shops which depend on these workers for custom are likely to have to close, adding not only to the unemployed but also to the general air of decay in the district.

TEST YOURSELF ON FACTS

1. List three causes of unemployment.
2. List three effects of unemployment.
3. List five purposes of leisure.

(B) LEISURE

1. How Do You Spend Your Leisure?

(a) Make a list of ways in which everyone in the class likes to spend leisure time. Then match them to the following categories:

   (i) Resting to recover from the weariness of work.
  (ii) Exercise which may be enjoyed for a number of reasons, e.g. health, restoring a sense of harmony, venting frustration through physical effort.
 (iii) Sharing relationships.
  (iv) Helping other people which also provides personal satisfaction for the helper.
   (v) Joining in activities with other people which provides a sense of belonging.
  (vi) Sitting slumped, bored and miserable.
 (vii) Dashing about in meaningless, feverish activity for fear of silence.
(viii) Earning money doing another job.
  (ix) Practising creative skills, e.g. music, painting.
   (x) Caring for animals.

(b) Add up how much time everyone in the class spends watching television and videos. Work out the average. How much of life will that represent by the age of 60 if viewing is continued at that rate?

One of the difficulties in providing for leisure is that making facilities available for a majority means that a minority has to work to provide them.

2. The Law
(a) 1986 Sunday Trading Bill
The government wanted to standardise regulations about Sunday opening of shops. For example at present newspapers and tobacco can be sold all day but the Sunday opening of bookstalls in cathedrals is illegal.

The Bill was defeated largely through the efforts of all the churches who mounted the Keep Sunday Special Campaign.

Do you think there is anything wrong in visiting a DIY shop or Garden Centre on Sunday? Should a minority who wish to worship on Sundays impose their views on those who do not?

Trade Unions were also concerned because of their duty to protect employees from being legally bound to work on rest days.

What would be the effect on family life if mothers had to work on Sundays?

Once *any* shop can open, *every* shop needs to do so in order to preserve its share of the market. Before long there is pressure for banks to open as well (as in Scotland), transport services have to be increased, more police are needed and there is no longer a day of rest for anyone.

(b) 1780 Sunday Observance Act
Under this Act it is illegal to take money at the gate for sporting events on Sundays.

How do sports promoters get round this law?

(c) Gaming and Lotteries Act
This Act forbids betting on Sundays. Horse racing is not much fun without betting so the issue of what is allowed on Sundays is likely to be before parliament in one form or another for some time to come and you need to make up your own minds over the conflicting claims of the two sides.

CHECK YOUR UNDERSTANDING
1. *What is the difference between unemployment and leisure?*
2. *What is meant by the 'knock-on' effect of unemployment?*
3. *Explain the views of (a) the Church, (b) Trade Unions on Sunday trading.*

CHRISTIAN PERSPECTIVES

SUGGESTIONS FOR BIBLE STUDY
Gen. 2.2–3; 4.9   Mark 6.31
Ex. 20.8–11

(A) UNEMPLOYMENT
As Christians regard work as part of God's plan for human beings, they believe that to deny people work is frustrating the will of God and is therefore sin. Furthermore the book of Genesis contains the well-known story of Cain murdering his brother Abel. *What does Cain reply when God asks him what has happened to his brother?*

WHAT DO YOU THINK?
1. Is the Church justified in questioning the morality of the huge gulf between the lives of the unemployed and those who have work or should it keep out of politics?
2. Should caring be expressed through (a) voluntary charitable giving by the 'haves' to the 'have nots', (b) taxation to sustain unemployment benefit levels, (c) political action to create new jobs?

(B) LEISURE
(a) Find the commandment which deals with the Sabbath. Copy it out and learn it.
(b) Read about Jesus' own attitude to times of leisure. He used to go away quietly to renew his relationship with the Father in prayer. It is clear that he expected his followers to do the same. A Christian perspective on the use of leisure will therefore include times of quiet in the belief that we are made up of body, mind and spirit and each of these parts of us needs renewing. Recreation then becomes truly re-creation.

COURSEWORK
Carry out a survey of the shops and leisure activities available on Sundays in your own area. If possible interview people who have to work on Sundays (*not* while they are trying to work!) and find out their views. Then interview people who use the facilities provided and find out how necessary they find them. Consult a minister of religion on his/her views. Then write at length on 'Problems and Possibilities in Sunday trading'.

Trade Units

TO START YOU TALKING

1. Should everyone belong to a Trade Union?
2. Should everyone have the right to strike?
3. Consider each of the following in turn and make up your own minds who suffers from their striking. Can these people influence the strike's outcome? If not, why should they suffer?

   Air traffic control officers: bakers: coal miners: nurses: printers: teachers: railway workers: undertakers.

INFORMATION

GLOSSARY

Make sure you understand the meanings of key words which appear in any discussion of Trade Union activity.

Blackleg. A person who works during a strike thus weakening its impact. The word was coined during a nineteenth century miners' strike when it was possible to identify those who had been down the pit by their coal-encrusted skin.

Closed shop. A factory or office which will only recruit employees who belong to a Union.

Picketing. Strikers are allowed to stand at the entrance to their workplace to try to dissuade others from working and the firm's customers from doing business with them during the strike.

Secondary picketing. Picketing at factories *other* than the one where the strike is taking place.

Shop floor. The workers in a factory.

Shop steward. The elected representative of a Trade Union in a place of work.

1. UNION MEMBERSHIP

The right to belong to a Trade Union was hard-won and grew out of the exploitation of workers during the nineteenth century. Joining a Trade Union was then a sign of solidarity with fellow workers who were fighting for a just cause. Full employment in recent decades has given great power to the unions which they have used to improve their own position as well as to negotiate profitable terms for their members. Until 1979 Trade Union membership rose steadily but numbers are now falling. This fall is linked to the rise in unemployment. At the end of 1987 10.5 million people were Trade Union members.

TEST YOURSELF ON FACTS
1. What is a closed shop?
2. What is secondary picketing?
3. What is the role of a shop steward?

2. REASONS FOR JOINING A TRADE UNION

Do you expect to join a Trade Union when you start work?

(a) Is a worker justified in accepting wage increases, redundancy payments, welfare benefits which have been negotiated by Trade Unions without supporting those Unions?

(b) Can an individual expect fair treatment in a dispute with an employer without Union representation?

(c) Health and safety at work are often monitored by Unions although an employer is legally responsible for them. Many processes and practices are dangerous and it would be difficult for an individual on his own to bring pressure to bear on an employer for improvements.

(d) Are employees laying themselves open to a possible crisis of conscience in undertaking to obey decisions of a Union which as individuals they might believe to be unjustified?

In pairs act the parts of a shop steward trying to persuade a new employee to join his Union.

3. CLOSED SHOP

In many industries Unions have agreements with management that they will only employ workers who belong to a Trade Union. This arrangement is supposed to lead to better relations between management and workers and make industrial bargaining simpler. On the other hand the closed shop makes Unions more powerful. There have been situations in which a closed shop agreement has been made and *existing* workers who have refused to join the Union have been sacked. A similar situation, though in reverse, arose at the Government Communications Headquarters (GCHQ). For security reasons the government found it necessary to ban Trade Union membership with its attendant risk of strikes. Employees were offered £1,000 (before tax) in compensation in return for giving up their Union membership. A tiny minority refused to do so. In the end they were sacked.

Is there any moral justification for the behaviour of both sides?

4. STRIKES

The 1984 Trade Union Act gives greater responsibility to the members of a Union in the calling of a strike. Its main provisions are:

(a) The governing body of the Union should be elected by members in a secret ballot. This makes it more difficult for extremists to gain control. A MORI poll conducted for *The Times* at the opening of the 1987 TUC Conference showed that 48 per cent of Trade Union members believed unions were controlled by extremists.

(b) The Union can only retain its legal immunity in organising a strike if a secret ballot is held over whether strike action should be taken.

WHAT DO YOU THINK?

1. Should the families of workers on strike receive social security benefits?
2. Does a Trade Union have an obligation to the community or only to its members? You need to think clearly about the relationship between unions and the community as a whole, remembering that members of trade unions are also members of the community.

---

5. PICKETING

The legal reason for picketing is 'peaceful persuasion'. Three aspects of picketing cause public concern:

(a) Mass picketing which seeks to prevent work continuing through sheer weight of numbers.
(b) Violence which changes 'peaceful persuasion' into intimidation.
(c) Secondary picketing and the use of 'flying pickets' to halt supplies.

CHECK YOUR UNDERSTANDING

1. *What is the legal purpose of picketing?*
2. *Why is it important for all Union members to play a full part in Union decision-making?*
3. *Write an essay of about 200 words on the Christian attitude to strikes.*

CHRISTIAN PERSPECTIVES

SUGGESTIONS FOR BIBLE STUDY
Matt. 20.1–16   Luke 10.7; 16.19–31
Eph. 4.26–27 1 Peter 2.13–15 Romans 13.1–5

The Christian caught up in Trade Union action has to seek to do the will of God. It is probable that different Christians will reach different conclusions. What matters is that they should have thought about the problem and come to a reasoned conclusion rather than merely following the crowd. Here are some pointers to a Christian perspective. Which of the Bible references applies in each case?

(a) *Reasonableness*
Jesus said that a worker earns his pay, but how would a shop steward react to the situation in the parable of the workers in the vineyard? Why might he object?

(b) *Justification*
The Christian will want to decide whether the suffering which a strike will cause can be justified. There may well be a case if the strike hurts an unjust employer more than anyone else but often innocent people who are powerless to influence events suffer most.

(c) *Representation*
A Christian is committed to obeying lawful authority. There have been times in the history of the Trade Union movement when it is questionable whether the leaders of the unions have genuinely represented the views of their members. Christians would therefore regard it as important to play a full part in the democratic process so that their influence is felt. Only then can the unions' decisions be treated as lawful authority.

(d) *Fairness*
Remember that one man's pay increase is another man's price rise. Work out a Christian view on pay claims.

(e) *Caring*
Christians acknowledge the supremacy of love in any argument and are committed to maintaining a caring relationship with those with whom they disagree.

COURSEWORK

Make a detailed study of any strike which occurs while you are working on this topic, paying particular attention to the following factors: reasons for the strike, the employers' position, the pre-strike ballot, picketing, effects on the public, result of the strike, the moral issues involved.

Then write at length about what happened.

TO START YOU THINKING

Check your own use of money

1. Add up how much you yourself received from all sources last week, e.g. from parents, regular job, casual earnings. Did you acquire any of it dishonestly? If so, why did you do it?

2. How did you spend your money? Divide your outgoings into money spent on yourself and money spent or given to others.

3. Consider this budget of an office worker starting a first job in London in 1990.
   Basic pay is £8,000. After deductions for tax and National Insurance, take-home pay is approximately £5,400. Fares to work cost £400. Part of a shared flat costs £3,000. Food and share of heating for the flat and telephone bills cost a further £1,500, leaving £500 for everything else. How would *you* allocate this money? You will probably find it easiest to calculate your annual expenditure on clothes, holidays and presents first and deduct that from the £500 and then work out the rest on a weekly basis.

Did you save anything? i.e. are you thrifty
Did you give anything to charity? How much?

INFORMATION

We all need money. Most of us would like to have more. The moral element hinges on our *attitude* to it. If we think too much of money and the material things it can provide we may turn into selfish, materialistic people with little or no concern for others.

Think for yourselves of *ten* specific ways in which the community uses money either for the common good or for people in need. This money is likely to come from one of two sources:

1. TAXATION

Taxation is a way of distributing money so that all may share in its benefits. Yet few pay taxes gladly and many go to considerable lengths to avoid them.

What is the difference between tax evasion and tax avoidance? Find out the standard rate of income tax and the level of income at which a single person is liable to pay at that rate.

2. CHARITIES

Charitable giving needs to go beyond the occasional emptying of small change into a collector's tin. Our taxation system encourages regular giving through **deeds of covenant**, i.e. when an individual promises to make regular gifts to a registered charity over a four year period, the charity is able to reclaim tax which has already been paid on that money thus increasing the donation.

These are good uses of money. The selfish use of money brings risks, e.g.

(a) Incentives which are aimed at people's natural greed and selfishness – more for *me* and *my* family – encourage the breakdown of society.

   Give examples. If you are stuck look again at Unit 21.

(b) There is a risk that we always want more yet never think we have enough. It is said that when John Wesley was a young man he had an income of £30 p.a. of which he needed £28 to live and so gave away £2. By the end of his life his income had risen to £120 but he still lived on £28 and gave the rest away.

   Apart from inflation, is there any reason why this should not happen today?

(c) The way in which money is made affects people. Huge sums could be made, for example, through drugs trafficking but few would envy the material prosperity of anyone making money out of human misery, and cynical disregard of human need inevitably affects the characters of those who make money in this kind of way.

WHAT DO YOU THINK?
How can money affect a person's character?

CHRISTIAN PERSPECTIVES

SUGGESTIONS FOR BIBLE STUDY
Matt. 6.19–24
Mark 10.17–27; 12.41–44
Luke 3.10–13; 12.16–21; 16.19–31
2 Corinth. 8 and 9
1 Tim. 6.10

St Paul wrote 'love of money is the root of all evil' (1 Tim. 6.10), i.e. it is not the money itself but our attitude to it which may become a problem. This idea runs right through the New Testament.

1. Sermon on the Mount (Matt. 6.19–24)

If a person sets his heart on material things he will put his energies into acquiring them and risks losing his sense of spiritual values.
Give examples of spiritual values.

2. Rich young man (Mark 10.17–27)

Jesus realises that it is the man's money which separates him from God by giving him a false sense of security. What does he say to the young man? Do you think these words are meant to be taken literally by everyone?
What other things, apart from money, might give a person a false sense of security?

3. Parable of the Rich Fool (Luke 12.16–21)

Read the story Jesus told when he was asked to settle a quarrel between two brothers over a will. Notice that the man in the story is entirely self-centred and had done nothing with his money which was of any value in the sight of God.
Give examples of what might have been of value in God's sight.

CHECK YOUR UNDERSTANDING
1. In what way does money give a sense of false security?
2. What did Jesus mean by 'How hard it will be for rich people to enter the kingdom of God.'?
3. Find out and explain the meaning of 'stewardship'.

4. Parable of the rich man and Lazarus (Luke 16.19–31)

The story is based on a Jewish folk tale so do not treat it as a geography of the next world.

Why is the rich man condemned? How might this apply in the modern world?

5. Sharing (Luke 3.10–13 and 2 Corinth. 8 and 9)

Read what John the Baptist tells people to do and then read St Paul's eloquent account of Gentile Christians making a collection to help Jewish Christians in Jerusalem. Then turn back to Unit 21 and read about *Faith in the City* and the Church Urban Fund. Can you see the connection?

In the Old Testament the book of Leviticus had laid down that Jews should offer one tenth (**a tithe**) of all they possess to God. St Paul makes it clear that Christian giving *is not fixed by rules* but is left to the individual and is a response of gratitude for God's goodness to them. Meanness then suggests that the individual is unaware of that goodness or is lacking in gratitude.

6. The widow's mite (Mark 12.41–44)

True generosity involves sacrifice and does not depend on the size of a person's bank balance.

TEST YOURSELF ON FACTS
1. What does St Paul say is the root of all evil? (*Be accurate*)
2. Complete the following quotation from the Sermon on the Mount: 'You cannot serve — and —'.
3. What is a tithe?
4. What is a deed of covenant?

COURSEWORK
From the information contained in this Unit make up your own minds about the morality of gambling and then write an essay expressing your views.

1. Try to imagine what the world would be like without rules. What advantages and disadvantages can you see? Would you really have greater freedom?
2. Could a community of individuals exist without rules (Look again at Unit 8). Notice that community rules put the good of the community before the wishes of the individual.
3. What principles would you use if you were left to draw up school rules? In what ways would your list of rules differ from the existing one? How would you deal with people who refused to keep them?

INFORMATION

1. LAWS

Statutory laws are rules agreed by the state for maintaining law and order. Breaking these laws with wrongful intent is crime.

There are two kinds of offence:

(a) Indictable, i.e. serious crimes like robbery, murder.
(b) Non-indictable, i.e. less serious crimes like parking offences.

2. CAUSES OF CRIME

If you have studied all the previous Units of this book you should by now have some insight into factors which can cause crime. They are likely to include the following:

(a) *Poverty* (Look again at Unit 21)
(b) *Poor housing* and overcrowding (Unit 21)
(c) *Unemployment* (Unit 23)
(d) *Boredom* and the failure of society to provide constructive outlets for frustrated young people (Unit 23)
(e) *Greed and envy.* Sociologists speak of **'relative deprivation'**, meaning that people feel deprived compared with those around them. Such people may develop unrealistic expectations fanned by advertising and fall for temptation.
(f) *Broken homes.* Law-abiding behaviour depends on consistent training and control. It is known that separation from parents can be more upsetting to a child than bereavement so look again at the problems discussed in Units 9 and 10, and relate them to the risk of delinquency.

(g) *Prejudice* of all kinds leading to the individual feeling an outsider (**alienation** is the technical term). Look at Units 17–20.
(h) *Personality difficulties.* Studies have shown that persistent adult offenders tend to be mentally abnormal and neurotic personalities.
(i) *Deterioration in moral standards.* It is known that the average young person in a deprived area will join in crime rather than be thought different. This kind of social pressure is exerted in many situations. Do you make life difficult for people who want to work in class? Why does this happen? Who is in the wrong if the individual cannot stand up to this kind of bullying?

WHAT DO YOU THINK?
What would you reply to someone who said 'Making allowance for criminals only increases crime'?

3. HELP FOR VICTIMS OF CRIME

(a) Compensation

Since 1964 it has been possible for people to receive compensation from government funds for criminal injury. Money cannot make up for the distress caused by crime but it is nevertheless of practical help to victims.

(b) National Association of Victim Support Schemes

This organisation started in Bristol in 1974. Volunteers are recruited to help victims of crime recover after the shock. They visit the victim as soon as possible after the crime and are able to offer support and advice. Many victims are likely to have to appear as witnesses in court and find the proceedings distressing. It is invaluable to be helped, possibly over a long period, by the friendship of someone who understands how they are feeling.

Find out whether there is a branch of this organisation in your own locality. If there is not, approach the local police to find out what other steps are being taken to help victims of crime.

CHECK YOUR UNDERSTANDING

1. What is the difference between indictable and non-indictable offences?

2. What is 'relative deprivation'?

3. What is the difference between crime and sin?

CHRISTIAN PERSPECTIVES

SUGGESTIONS FOR BIBLE STUDY

Ex. 20.1–17   Romans 13.1–5
Mark 12.29–31

---

1. The Ten Commandments

The laws by which God's people are to live are set out in the ten commandments (Unit 2, p. 5), traditionally passed on to them by Moses at Mount Sinai. They are moral absolutes.

2. Jesus' Summary of the Law

Look up what he said in Mark 12.29–31. Copy out the words and learn them.

3. Romans 13.1–5

When St Paul wrote his letter to Christians in Rome the Roman authorities were pagan and it was a Roman governor who had ordered the crucifixion of Jesus less than thirty years earlier. So Christians must have been startled by Paul's wholehearted backing for Roman law. Nor does Paul rule out the possibility of state persecution of Christians, yet he still insists that the State authorities hold their authority from God. This belief is still enshrined in our own coronation ceremonies.

Can you think of circumstances in which a Christian might find himself bound to disobey the law?

4. Crime and Sin

Make sure you understand the difference between crime and sin. Crime is breaking the law; sin is 'missing the mark', i.e. failing to live up to God's standard.

The Church for centuries has identified seven deadly sins, i.e. sins which, if persisted in, will eventually kill the soul. They are pride, covetousness, lust, anger, gluttony, envy, sloth. *Are any of these crimes?*

Although many sins are not crimes, sin is just as damaging to the community. Crime upsets the stability of society whereas Christians believe that sin upsets a relationship with God and other people. Crime and sin need different treatment which we shall consider in the next Unit.

TEST YOURSELF ON FACTS

1. What are the seven deadly sins?
2. What is the second great commandment quoted by Jesus?
3. What is the National Association of Victim Support Scheme?

COURSEWORK

Write an essay on Christian perspectives on the causes of crime. You will need to refer to previous Units which have considered the various issues in greater detail.

TO START YOU TALKING

When people break the law society punishes them because crime upsets the ordered life of everyone. Unless the punishment reflects society's concern for the victims of crime it is felt to be unfair. Until recently rape was not punished as severely in this country as women felt it should be but it takes time for public opinion to make itself felt.

What punishment would you regard as appropriate in the following cases?

Football hooliganism: rape: robbery with violence: vandalism: evading paying fares on public transport: causing death on the road through careless driving: kidnapping: murder.

Are you basing your ideas on emotion or have you a purpose in mind?

INFORMATION

1. PURPOSE OF PUNISHMENT

Punishment has four purposes. Sometimes one dominates, sometimes another, but most sentences are a mixture of several. They are:

(a) **Vengeance**

In earliest times an injured person was entitled to go out and take whatever revenge he liked. Moses set a limit on revenge with his law 'eye for eye and tooth for tooth'.

(b) **Retribution**

This means that revenge is taken right out of the hands of the victim and is dealt with independently, i.e. by the court. Its purpose is symbolised by the statue of Justice which adorns the roof of the Central Criminal Court in London. She carries a sword representing judicial authority, scales and is blindfold. Justice must be impartial, uninfluenced by appearances.

(c) **Deterrence**

It is felt that 'soft' sentences encourage crime and that severe sentences act as a deterrent but is it morally right to punish a criminal more severely than deserved in order to deter others? People with experience in this field tell us that the only really effective deterrent is the certainty of being found out.

(d) **Reform**

Here the emphasis shifts from punishment to helping the criminal become a normal law-abiding citizen. In the long-term, society is best served by treatment which reforms criminals but most people still feel that concern for the criminal weakens sympathy for the victims. *What do you think?*

Reform is unlikely to happen, except in rare cases, in the degrading conditions which are to be found in our overcrowded prisons. In 1986 the number of prisoners confined in twos or threes in cells designed for one person reached 18.4 thousand.

The Report of the Archbishop of Canterbury's Commission on Urban Priority Areas (*Faith in the City*) describes conditions where 'owing to the scarcity of work and educational facilities more prisoners spend the greater part of their time, and many 24 hours of the day, locked in cells. These conditions are insanitary and degrading, and we were shocked to find that they have become a normal part of a prison sentence.'

If society wishes to reform criminals it must find a more effective way than imprisonment.

2. KINDS OF PUNISHMENT

These are the punishments available to the courts:

(a) Attendance Centres

Offenders can be made to attend on Saturdays for up to three hours at a time. The Centres are intended for those aged 10–16 but some cater for people aged 17–20.

What do you think is the aim of this punishment?

(b) Probation orders

These apply only for people aged 17 + . The function of the probation officer is to 'advise, assist and befriend' the offender. The offender remains at liberty but this treatment only works if he/she is prepared to co-operate.

What benefits can you see for (i) the offender, (ii) society in probation orders?

(c) Community Service

Offenders over the age of 17 who have been found guilty of an offence which carries a prison sentence can instead be made to do unpaid work for a number of hours varying between totals of 40 and 240 hours.

(d) Youth Custody Centres

These have been a controversial and not very successful form of punishment. The intention was to keep young people out of prison but there is a high rate of re-offending by people who have been sent to the Centres. They were intended for 15–20-year-olds to give them a 'short, sharp shock' for a minimum of four months to be followed by supervision by a probation officer.

What weaknesses can you see in this punishment?

(e) Imprisonment

The United Kingdom imprisons a higher proportion of its population than any other major country in Western Europe yet the crime rate for 1988 showed a five per cent decrease over the previous year. Prisoners may be let off a third of their sentence for good conduct. From the point of view of the prison service this is an aid to discipline. *What benefit might it have for a person in prison?*

(f) Suspended sentences

These only take effect if the convicted person is found guilty of another offence which carries a prison sentence during the period of the suspended sentence. *In what circumstances do you think a judge might choose this form of punishment?*

(g) Fines

Do you regard fines as a fair punishment? Should they be related to the level of a person's income or only to the seriousness of the offence?

TEST YOURSELF ON FACTS
1. What is the function of a probation officer?
2. What is a suspended sentence?
3. Name three purposes of punishment.
4. Give four causes of crime.
5. In Romans 13, what does Paul say sums up the commandments?

CAPITAL PUNISHMENT

From time to time parliament considers re-introducing capital punishment for certain crimes notably murder. *What do you think?* Here are some ideas to start you off:

'Life is sacred. Anyone who takes life should pay with his own.'

'If the victim's life is sacred so is the murderer's.'

'A person can take life in self-defence so society can take the life of a criminal who is a threat to the community.'

'Without a death penalty murder is treated too lightly.'

'What about the effect on those involved? Would you be prepared to be hangman? What about the doctor, the priest, the prison governor and staff, even the Home Secretary?'

'Can we be certain mistakes are never made? Once a man is hanged he can't be brought back to life.'

'The death penalty protects society from criminals.'

'The death penalty acts as a deterrent.'

WHAT DO YOU THINK?

Debate the motion 'This house believes that the death penalty should be restored in cases of crimes of violence.'

CHRISTIAN PERSPECTIVES

SUGGESTIONS FOR BIBLE STUDY

Gen. 9.5–6	Matt. 5.7; 18.21–35
Ex. 21.24	Luke 15.11–32
Romans 13	

Christians distinguish between the demands of justice and the need for mercy and forgiveness.

1. JUSTICE

The law of Moses had been an advance on the unlimited revenge previously allowed and St Paul did not recommend being soft with offenders.

2. MERCY

The teaching of Jesus is responsible for a new element in Christian thinking. One of the Beatitudes (Matt. 5.6) – eight sayings which put in a nutshell the teaching of the Sermon on the Mount – highlights the need for mercy, and in the parable of the Unforgiving Servant, Jesus reminds his disciples of their own indebtedness to God for his mercy to them.

CHECK YOUR UNDERSTANDING

1. *In what way was Moses' law 'eye for eye and tooth for tooth' an advance in its time?*
2. *Why are Christians bound to show mercy?*
3. *What part do you think should be played by (a) justice, (b) mercy, (c) forgiveness, in dealing with crime?*

---

3. FORGIVENESS

Christians believe that God does something which no court of law could do – lets the guilty go free and treats them as though they are righteous – and he does this purely out of love. No amount of good works can *earn* this freedom. Christians believe that the price for it was paid by Jesus on the cross. It is God's free gift. Nevertheless people have to make it their own by repentance. If someone wants to give you a five pound note, it does not become your own unless you put out your hand and accept it. The parable of the Prodigal Son shows God's way in action.

Forgiveness must not be lightly regarded as the solution to the problem of crime. Of course Christians must forgive but it is a costly virtue which makes heroic demands on those called to show it. Victims may manage to forgive their assailants; it is not for the court to do so on their behalf. Crime is dealt with through justice tempered by mercy; sin through repentance and forgiveness. Both justice and forgiveness are expressions of love and it is this virtue above all others which reflects the Christian response to the problems discussed in this Unit.

COURSEWORK

Someone has written to your local paper advocating bringing back corporal punishment for crimes of violence. Think carefully what arguments might have been used then write to the editor expressing your own views and taking up the points made in the first letter.

UNIT 28 Church & State. Civil Disobedience

TO START YOU TALKING

1. Are the following issues political, religious, both political *and* religious or neither?

   Abortion: building motorways: conditions in prisons: defence: education: euthanasia: experiments on animals: pensions: space research: unemployment.

2. Should the Church keep out of politics?

A meeting of the General Synod of the Church of England at Church House, London.

INFORMATION

It is no secret that Church and government in Britain today do not see eye to eye. Bishops are criticised for 'meddling' in politics and at the same time for failing to make moral pronouncements. No one party has a monopoly of religious insights and there are religious people of most persuasions on both sides of Parliament, so how is conflict to be resolved?

1. REASONS FOR CONFLICT

Copy out the following statements in rough and give yourself five boxes or columns beside each headed 'Strongly agree', 'Agree', 'Don't know', 'Disagree', 'Strongly disagree'. Then tick in the appropriate place:

(a) The function of the Church is a purely spiritual one and they should stick to it.
(b) The function of the State is to govern without interference.
(c) The Church is committed to service.
(d) Politicians are motivated by a desire for power.
(e) The Church must give a clear lead on moral issues.
(f) The State must compromise to meet the wishes of as many people as possible.
(g) The Church should limit its work to caring for individuals.
(h) The State must function through structured organisations and cannot take account of individuals.
(i) The Church is answerable to God for its use of authority.
(j) The State is only answerable to the people for its use of power.

From the notes you have made, make your own list of reasons for conflict between Church and parliament.

2. METHODS OF INVOLVEMENT

Three ways of involvement are available to everyone:

(a) **The ballot box.** It is essential to vote as soon as you are old enough. Go to public meetings and ask parliamentary candidates their views on moral issues. Make your own views known.

(b) **Pressure groups.** Many have been mentioned in this book. Show your concern by joining like-minded people to press your case.

(c) **Writing to your MP.** Members of Parliament are your representatives whether or not you voted for their party.

HOUSE OF COMMONS
LONDON SW1A 0AA

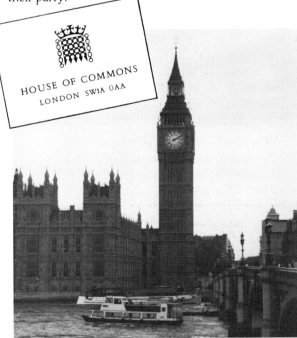

3. CIVIL DISOBEDIENCE

A fourth way of making views known is civil disobedience. This needs very careful thought and you have to be certain of three things:

(a) that all other ways of changing a bad law are closed to you;
(b) that you are prepared to accept the consequences;
(c) that the law you are breaking is so wrong that you are justified in not submitting to authority.

Civil disobedience must not be thought of as right in itself. In this country you are most likely to meet it in the context of the Campaign for Nuclear Disarmament, perhaps at Greenham Common or Molesworth.

There is also the Peace Tax Campaign. Forty-five per cent of tax is spent on a defence policy based on a nuclear deterrent. Some members of the campaign have withheld payment of income tax unless a 'non-armaments fund' is established, since they are opposed in conscience to nuclear arms. The Tax Inspectors have refused their request on the grounds that tax is levied by parliament and that opposition must be expressed through parliament.

Probably the greatest exponent of civil disobedience in the twentieth century was Mahatma Gandhi (see p. 74). His use of this 'weapon' contributed to the ending of British rule in India. Read his life for yourselves before making up your own mind.

CHRISTIAN PERSPECTIVES

Christians in politics experience tension between party policy and Christian faith. On moral issues, for example capital punishment, abortion, it is customary to allow a free vote in the House but on other issues, for example defence policy, an MP has to toe the party line. Nevertheless the Christian has certain guidelines to help make decisions where religion and politics seem to conflict.

1. The Incarnation
Christians believe that in Jesus God himself took human life. God is therefore involved in material as well as spiritual things and Christians believe that the two cannot be separated.

2. Teaching of Jesus
(a) *Matt. 22.21*
Jesus was asked a catch question about whether Jews should pay taxes to the Roman authorities. What did he reply? He makes it clear that, *provided duty to God is not infringed*, his followers are to obey lawful authority. Sometimes it will be difficult to decide whether a particular action of the state infringes an individual's duty to God. Then different people will come to different conclusions in good faith. What matters is that the issue should be confronted and a decision made rather than blindly accepting the decision of others.

(b) *Matt. 25.31–46*
What guidance does this parable give which is relevant to the issue of Christian involvement in politics?

3. St Paul
Read Romans 13 again very carefully. Remember that, for Christians, all lawful authority comes from God and must be respected. Occasionally there is no choice but disobeying the law. In the New Testament, for example, we read of Peter and John being told to stop preaching about the Resurrection. They continue doing so, are re-arrested and Peter tells the Court 'We must obey God rather than men' (Acts 5.29).

Mahatma Gandhi

(If possible hire the film 'Gandhi').

Gandhi, a Hindu, has been compared to Jesus. He was the greatest exponent of the power of non-violence in the twentieth century. He was born in 1869 in Gujurat on the West coast of India. At the age of 12 he was married to Kasturbai, also aged 12, by whom he eventually had four sons. She stood by him throughout his stormy life and died while in prison with him in 1944.

When he was 18 he decided to study law in London. The change of environment was almost overwhelming and, at first, he reacted by trying to adopt European customs – all except meat-eating. He had promised his mother to retain the vegetarianism of his Hindu faith and kept that promise. When he found that, despite adopting Western dress and taking lessons in Western social graces, he was still not accepted, he reverted to Indian dress and customs which he retained as far as possible for the rest of his life. Once qualified, he found work in South Africa but soon came up against racial discrimination in the law.

A journey from Durban to Pretoria in 1893 became a turning point in his life. The booking clerk had sold the young Indian lawyer a first class train ticket, but he was ordered into the van for coloured people at the back of the train. He refused to go, was removed by police and eventually continued his journey by stagecoach. Even then he was not allowed to travel inside the coach and was humiliated by the coachman. His mind was made up. He would fight laws which discriminated against coloured people.

During the Zulu rebellion of 1906 Gandhi established teams of Indian ambulancemen to help both sides. He was upset to find the British ill-treating Zulus and refusing to help their wounded and resolved he must devote his life to serving mankind.

The following year the Asiatic Registration Bill required all Indian citizens to be finger-printed and to carry a registration certificate. Under Gandhi's leadership a Passive Resistance Association was formed. It marked the beginning of his use of *Satyagraha* (= passive resistance).

Gandhi was later to explain that this was a method for attaining justice through *self*-sacrifice. Armed resistance uses body force; passive resistance uses soul force. The principle had close links with another Hindu principle – *ahimsa* – a refusal to harm any living thing. It is the victim who suffers in passive resistance and that suffering, freely accepted, exerts moral power.

Gandhi and his supporters burned their registration certificates and were sent to prison. Anti-Indian laws were tightened. When released Gandhi led marches, organised meetings and set out to fill the prisons to overflowing with those prepared to follow his example. By 1914 a compromise had been agreed with the government and Gandhi, now aged 45, felt free to return to India.

His first intervention in Indian politics came in 1917 in a wages dispute between mill-owners and workers. The workers claimed a fifty per cent increase. The owners offered twenty per cent and refused Gandhi's compromise suggestion of thirty-five per cent. He therefore undertook a public fast. After three days the owners accepted his suggestion. It was the first of eighteen occasions when Gandhi was to use fasting to achieve justice. He made it clear that this weapon could only be used effectively in a just cause.

At the end of World War I the British government failed to repeal restrictive wartime measures in India and Gandhi ordered a twenty-four hours' strike during which *workers were to spend their time in fasting and prayer.* Despite his orders there were outbreaks of violence culminating in a brutal massacre at Amritsar. Gandhi, realising that many of his followers were not morally strong enough to share his use of *satyagraha*, called off his campaign. It was at this

period that people began to address him as 'Mahatma' (= Great Soul).

During the twenties he worked hard to improve relations between Hindus and Muslims in India and in 1924 fasted for three weeks for this cause. He was also concerned about the treatment of 'Untouchables' (the lowest of the five castes in the Indian caste system).

The next major conflict with the British arose over the 1930 Salt Laws. The government, which controlled the salt mines, forbade Indians to make salt and levied a tax on this essential commodity. Gandhi led a great march to the coast gathering crowds as he went. He arrived at Dandi on 5th April, spent the night in prayer and, next morning, waded into the sea, collecting the water in shallow pans as the first step in making salt. The government ignored his action knowing they would be made to look ridiculous but as Gandhi's campaign spread and thousands followed his example around the coasts of India he was once again arrested and the prisons again began to overflow with thousands of his followers. Gandhi spent the time in prison fasting on behalf of the Untouchables. Hindu leaders dared not leave him to die and a compromise was worked out. When he was released he renewed his efforts to improve relations between Hindus and Muslims.

In August 1942 Congress passed a resolution that Britain must quit India. Gandhi, now aged 72, launched a campaign of civil disobedience in support of the resolution. Again he was imprisoned and again fasted as an appeal to God. There was an outcry for his release. Gandhi in prison was as much trouble to the government as Gandhi out of prison but he was not freed until May 1944 following the death in prison of his wife.

India became independent in 1947. Amid mounting turmoil between Hindus and Muslims, Gandhi again fasted for peace. He was saddened by the division of the continent into two separate nations, India and Pakistan.

In January 1948 he was shot at point blank range as he was going to a prayer meeting. His assassin, a young Hindu fanatic, believed Gandhi's life's work had led to India being lost to Hindus. Later generations have recognised that India, far from being 'lost', in fact *found* its true stature as a nation through the life of this remarkable man.

UNIT 29 — Just War Tradition. Crusades

TO START YOU TALKING

1. Why do individuals quarrel and fight? Try to think of particular situations in your own experience.

2. Why do nations go to war? Relate your ideas to particular examples.

3. Is there anything the individual can do to prevent war?

INFORMATION

In the past forty years, i.e. since the end of the Second World War, over 40 million people have died in wars. Peace is obviously hard to maintain and ordinary people the world over are anxious that war might break out again. It has always been so, but the existence of nuclear weapons invites us to look afresh at an ancient tradition which was originally intended to limit the effects of war.

1. THE JUST WAR TRADITION

The 'just war' tradition was never intended to *justify* war. War itself is always evil. The intention of this code was to put restraints on war and so limit the harm suffered. Although now generally regarded as a Christian tradition, it has its origins in much earlier Greek ideas. There is therefore nothing in the tradition itself which could not be accepted by a moral human being of any religion or none.

At its heart is the belief that moral standards apply even in war. Those fighting are still human beings possessing the knowledge of right and wrong which is common to us all. The 'just war' tradition provides guidance for them in the difficult decisions which have to be made about war. Remember that, even if all the conditions for a just war are met, *the war itself does not become good.*

When you are trying to decide whether a war is 'just' you have to consider these six conditions:

(a) Just cause

The cause of the war must be just. Article 31 of the United Nations Charter says that the only just cause for going to war is to defend oneself against an aggressor.

(b) Last resort

All other ways of settling the dispute must have been tried before going to war. For example, has every channel of diplomacy been used to reach a settlement?

(c) Chance of success

There must be a reasonable hope of success. When a nation is hopelessly outnumbered by the aggressor and has no hope of victory, the harm caused by war could be greater than that caused by surrender.

(d) Principle of proportion

War should not inflict *more* suffering than would be experienced by *not* going to war. This calculation is of particular importance in the debate on the use of nuclear arms. However, one cannot really know the extent of suffering which might have to be endured by not going to war.

(e) Right intention

The intention of those going to war must be right and achieving peace needs to be the prime aim.

Think of three reasons for going to war which would not meet this criterion.

(f) Safety of non-combatants

Civilians should not be intentionally attacked. This last condition was added in the Middle Ages. It still applies in the nuclear debate.

In other words, the cost of every act of war should be carefully calculated in advance. The standards to be applied are *moral* ones rather than mere self-interest.

Do you think this degree of forethought is possible in war?

CHECK YOUR UNDERSTANDING
1. What was the intention of the 'just war' tradition?
2. What is a crusade?

---

2. CRUSADES

Sometimes a nation is led to believe that all right is on its side and that the enemy is entirely wrong, i.e. that it is fighting on God's side to destroy *God's* enemies. If this happens the war has become a **crusade**. Think of an example of such a war (apart from the wars to which we give the name the Crusades).

Two questions have to be faced:

(a) How can anyone know for sure that all right is on his side?
(b) Can religion ever justify killing?

War is normally the result of failures on both sides and it is seldom that one side is entirely right and the other entirely wrong.

TEST YOURSELF ON FACTS

1. List six conditions of a just war.
2. List five conditions for peace.

---

3. CONDITIONS FOR PEACE

War breaks out when conditions for peaceful co-existence break down. These conditions are:

(a) Well-defined and acceptable boundaries.
(b) Adequate food and raw materials.
(c) Mutual tolerance and economic co-operation.
(d) A government which is reasonably acceptable to its people.
(e) A population with sufficient education to think out for themselves the consequences of aggression.

WHAT DO YOU THINK?

Why doesn't God stop wars?

CHRISTIAN PERSPECTIVES

SUGGESTIONS FOR BIBLE STUDY
Matt. 5.9; 5.38–42   Luke 10.25–37

It is all too easy to take Bible quotations out of context and use them as ammunition in the debate about war and peace but, if they are to be rightly understood, you need to know something about the times in which they were written.

1. OLD TESTAMENT

There was almost constant war in ancient Israel and the Israelites believed that God would protect them because they were his Chosen People. In fact priests went off to war with the troops.

The prophets tried to steer them away from putting their trust in military power but without much success.

2. NEW TESTAMENT

(a) Matt. 5.38–42

At his Temptations Jesus rejected political power as the right way of doing God's will. He was not a military Messiah and taught his followers about the claims of love.

(b) Matt. 5.9

Sometimes the seventh Beatitude is quoted in discussions about the Christian view on War and Peace but care must be taken in interpreting these words. Peace is much more than absence of war. The Greek word for peace is *eirene* and the Hebrew word *shalom*. Both these words include both material and spiritual values – prosperity, serenity and fellowship. Everyone loves peace but the peace *maker* is likely to suffer unpopularity and even pain in order to achieve *shalom*.

(c) Luke 10.25–37

Can you imagine the Good Samaritan arriving on the scene while the robbers were still beating up their victim and doing nothing? Would this have been the way of love?

COURSEWORK

1. Choose any three wars, either from history or our own times, and analyse how far they measure up to the standards of the 'just war' tradition.

   To start you off, make six columns, one for each of the 'just war' conditions and taking each of the wars you have chosen in turn, consider it from the point of view of *each side*. Tick the appropriate column in each case. Once you have this basic material, present your findings in as interesting a way as possible.

2. Get hold of a recording of Britten's War Requiem and if possible ask music staff to introduce you to it. Britten blends the words of the Mass for the Dead with poetry inspired by war. The idiom may seem strange at first but most people of your age quickly become interested and absorbed in the work. Then express your own reaction to the music in whatever way seems appropriate – poetry, prose, painting, drama, dance.

TO START YOU TALKING

1. Can the use of nuclear weapons ever be justified?
2. Which is the greater catastrophe – having to go to war to defend one's country or living under the occupation of an enemy power?

INFORMATION

1. NUCLEAR WAR

Once nuclear weapons have been invented they are bound to form part of any defence strategy. The dilemma arises in deciding whether their possession makes war more or less likely. Nuclear defence strategy is based on Mutual Assured Destruction, known by the telling acronym MAD.

(a) Deterrence

The debate about nuclear weapons hinges on their power as a deterrent. Nevertheless not even a defensive use of nuclear weapons can fulfil all the criteria of the 'just war' tradition (Unit 29). *Work out for yourselves which 'just war' conditions could not apply in a nuclear war.* Can a nation which respects that tradition morally even *possess* nuclear weapons as a deterrent? If there is no intention of ever using them, their possession is a matter of enormously expensive bluff since it is necessary for a potential enemy to believe that they would be used.

Smoke billowing 20,000 ft above Nagasaki after the atomic bomb raid in World War II.

WHAT DO YOU THINK?
A DEBATE: 'This House believes that Britain should ban all nuclear weapons from its soil.'

At break or lunch-time ask ten people for their views on whether this country should possess nuclear weapons. Some of these points of view may help to start you off:

Arguments in favour of nuclear deterrent
  (i) It works. There has been no war in Europe for over forty years.
 (ii) If nuclear weapons deter, can they then really be regarded as totally evil?
(iii) Possession of a nuclear deterrent may be the lesser of two evils without being good in itself.
 (iv) It is a stage along the road to disarmament when sufficient trust has been built up between opposing sides.
  (v) The purpose of the nuclear deterrent is to *prevent* war and to keep the peace.

Arguments against a nuclear deterrent
  (i) The vast and growing number of nuclear weapons makes war more likely.
 (ii) The use of weapons of mass destruction would be a moral outrage because civilians would be included on a huge scale. Far more would be killed than would be justified by any possible good result. No one could win such a war.
(iii) The money could be better spent on the Third World.
 (iv) Mutual fear is hindering disarmament.

CHECK YOUR UNDERSTANDING
1. Give four reasons in favour of a nuclear deterrent.
2. Give four reasons against possessing a nuclear deterrent.
3. What is the meaning of
   (a) unilateralism, (b) multilateralism?

2. DISARMAMENT

The whole world can see that we have no need of the vast numbers of nuclear weapons stored around our planet. There are two possible ways of disarmament:

(a) Unilateralism

Some people believe that if one side renounces all nuclear weapons the other side will follow suit. They argue that it is mutual distrust which holds both sides back. Others fear that such action would leave all power on one side rather than leading to a just peace.

(b) Multilateralism

Others believe that abandoning nuclear weapons without adequate safeguards leads to the risk of nuclear blackmail. They therefore put their faith in the long, slow business of negotiating a mutual reduction of nuclear forces.

Investigate what is being done in this field at the time you are studying this Unit.

CHRISTIAN PERSPECTIVES

> ### SUGGESTIONS FOR BIBLE STUDY
> Ex. 15.3   Matt. 5.38–42
> Psalm 24.1   Romans 12.17–21

Christians are to be found on all sides of the nuclear debate and, although Biblical texts can be bandied about by all sides, they cannot provide a clear-cut answer.

(a) Ex. 15.3

A popular text used by those who wish to find biblical justification for going to war comes from Ex. 15.3, which is part of a great song of triumph after the Exodus of the Israelites from Egypt. Miriam sings 'The Lord is a warrior; the Lord is his name'. Hence war cannot be totally opposed to God's will in all circumstances.

(b) Matt. 5.38–42; Romans 12.17–21

Those who oppose the use of force would quote the Sermon on the Mount and St Paul's letter to the Romans which both teach love of enemies. To this over-riding pressure on Christians to love, the Bishop of Oxford, Richard Harries, replies 'the first step in loving a bully or a criminal is to stop him in his tracks'. (*Christianity and War in a Nuclear Age*, Mowbray). Only by bringing home to people the consequences of their actions can moral progress be made.

(c) Ps. 24.1

In the nuclear debate you also need to consider the question of man's use of his responsibility for the world's resources since nuclear war would bring about their annihilation. To whom does the psalmist say the earth belongs?

(d) The Church and the Bomb

In 1982 a Commission set up by the Church of England under the chairmanship of John Austin Baker, Bishop of

Salisbury, published an important report entitled *The Church and the Bomb*. It recommended that Britain should give up all its nuclear weapons and emphasised that disarmament negotiations were the best way of relieving the world of the threat of war.

The General Synod of the Church of England rejected the idea of unilateral disarmament but made it clear that it was Church policy to use every opportunity to work for peace. They urged the government to keep Britain's nuclear weapons for defensive use only saying that the Church of England could not agree to a policy which permitted 'first strike' use.

(e) Gaudium et Spes

An earlier Roman Catholic document, *Gaudium et Spes* (1965) had called for a total ban on nuclear weapons and a multilateral reduction in stocks of nuclear warheads. It pointed out that nuclear tests posed a threat to life and urged an end to the arms race.

> ### TEST YOURSELF ON FACTS
> 1. What recommendation did the Commission under the Bishop of Salisbury make in *The Church and the Bomb* with regard to this country's nuclear weapons?
> 2. What decision did the General Synod come to?
> 3. What does the Roman Catholic document *Gaudium et Spes* say on the subject of nuclear weapons?

> ### COURSEWORK
> Find out all you can about Hiroshima and then write at length on the subject 'Hiroshima – the facts and their influence.'

UNIT 31 Pacifism. Non-violence. Terrorism

TO START YOU TALKING

1. Think of five situations in which even a convinced pacifist might not be able to stick to his principles. Then pool your ideas and discuss the effectiveness of pacifism in these hard situations.
2. In a democracy does anyone have the right to oppose laws passed by an elected majority?

INFORMATION

1. PACIFISM

Read about Gandhi and Martin Luther King. Pacifism and non-violent action may then seem the most moral way through the dilemma of how to resist aggression in a nuclear age. However, it is worth remembering the advice given to the British Foreign Secretary by Hitler in 1937 – shoot Gandhi and your troubles in India will soon die out. Gandhi and Martin Luther King succeeded at least in part because they lived in an environment where religious values were largely respected. Nevertheless pacifism is an alternative to war and pacifists believe that the ending of all war is possible. They express their belief through being **conscientious objectors**, i.e. refusing to fight if their country goes to war.

2. SOCIETY OF FRIENDS

One of the best known societies dedicated to pacifism is the Society of Friends (Quakers). They were founded in 1652 under the leadership of George Fox and are committed to peace and reconciliation. In 1660 Quakers presented a Declaration to King Charles II which included the words ... *'We utterly deny all outward wars and strife, and fightings with outward weapons, for any end, or under any pretence whatever; this is our testimony to the whole world. The Spirit of Christ by which we are guided is not changeable, so as once to command us from a thing as evil, and again to move unto it; and we certainly know, and testify to the world, that the Spirit of Christ, which leads us into all truth, will never move us to fight and war against any man with outward weapons, neither for the Kingdom of Christ, nor for the Kingdom of the world.'*

3. EFFECTS OF PACIFISM

The pacifist has to accept the consequences of his attitude. In wartime the consequences may well be painful. Life is seldom made easy for those refusing military service. Quakers formed the Friends' Ambulance Unit to help their members make a positive life-*giving* contribution in times of war. Their services were needed in the front line, silencing the jibe of cowardice which is sometimes levelled against pacifists. Many pacifists were employed in civilian relief work overseas or did menial work in hospitals at home. Others drove ambulances or organised bomb shelters in cities.

The Red Cross provides another outlet for service for conscientious objectors (see p. 81).

4. NON-VIOLENCE

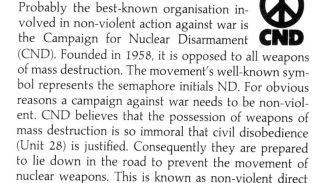

Probably the best-known organisation involved in non-violent action against war is the Campaign for Nuclear Disarmament (CND). Founded in 1958, it is opposed to all weapons of mass destruction. The movement's well-known symbol represents the semaphore initials ND. For obvious reasons a campaign against war needs to be non-violent. CND believes that the possession of weapons of mass destruction is so immoral that civil disobedience (Unit 28) is justified. Consequently they are prepared to lie down in the road to prevent the movement of nuclear weapons. This is known as non-violent direct action (NVDA).

Less dramatic but equally determined is the campaign pursued week by week all over the country. The publications department produces books, leaflets and a monthly magazine explaining CND's point of view. National demonstrations are organised – marches, human chains holding hands, vigils. Regular contact with MPs is maintained to ensure that CND's opinions remain in politicians' minds. Nuclear-free zones are encouraged. In these areas local councils have declared opposition to any siting or transportation of nuclear weapons within their boundaries.

You have to make up your own minds over these issues. Whether or not you agree with everything CND stands for you can learn a lot from them about the power of NVDA.

TEST YOURSELF ON FACTS

1. What is a conscientious objector?
2. Who are the Quakers?
3. What is CND?
4. What is a nuclear free zone?

CHECK YOUR UNDERSTANDING

1. Think of one specifically Christian reason for being a pacifist and one reason which anyone might uphold.
2. Give three non-violent ways of making your views known.

5. TERRORISM

An alternative way of making minority views known is through terrorism and you need to consider the morality of various ways of dealing with it. Terrorist tactics are used to undermine public confidence in the state and the rule of law. In this way terrorists hope to lower morale and resistance to their demands.

Think of some examples of terrorist tactics.

Most governments, publicly at least, are united in resisting terrorist demands on the grounds that giving in to blackmail raises the stakes. Consequently innocent people have to be put at risk. Danger comes when a nation's nerve gives way. Both the United States and France have been criticised for giving in to domestic pressures to save hostages in the Middle East.

> ### WHAT DO YOU THINK?
> Is it possible to resist terrorists' demands? Would it make any difference to your views if the victims were members of your own family?

CHRISTIAN PERSPECTIVES

> ### SUGGESTIONS FOR BIBLE STUDY
> Ex. 20.13   Matt. 26.51–52
> Jer. 38

1. PACIFISM

Not all Christians are pacifists and not all pacifists are Christians but some of the reasons given by pacifists for their beliefs are based on the Bible.

(a) Old Testament
(i) *Ex. 20.13*
Killing is specifically forbidden in the ten commandments. However, you need to know that there are eight different Hebrew words meaning 'to kill' but all with slightly different shades of meaning. The word used in this context is best translated 'murder', i.e. it is the *motive* as much as the deed which is important. Some people would argue that when society as a whole orders killing for its own safety it is not a case of murder.

(ii) *Jeremiah 38*
This is a famous case of God ordering non-resistance. Jeremiah was in the besieged city of Jerusalem in the year 586 BC. The king of Judah, Zedekiah, was a weak man and had no hope of resisting the Chaldean army. The prophet Jeremiah brought him the message from God that his people should surrender without fighting. Naturally Jeremiah was not popular with the officers of the Judean army. What did they do with him? Notice that the prophet stood his ground, refused to compromise his message and was prepared to pay the price himself, if necessary with his own life.

(b) New Testament
Some arguments in favour of pacifism are based specifically on the New Testament, e.g.

(i) The power of God's love is seen on the cross. Christian pacifists recognise this as God's way of reconciliation. As Jesus did not take up arms to defend himself nor will they. *Do you think Jesus was a pacifist?*

(ii) *Matt. 26.51–52*
We know from St John's gospel that it was Peter who cut off the ear. Jesus here seems to be giving him specific instructions against the use of force.

2. TERRORISM

It is easy to interpret a nation's concern for its kidnap victims as a response of love but it is not as straightforward as that. Of course emotions cry out to help them but the love of God was shown in the sacrifice of Jesus on the cross. Christians are called to follow him. Before he left on his last mission, Terry Waite made it clear that, should he be taken hostage, no bargains should be struck with evil men to obtain his release whatever the cost. The cost in human suffering both to himself, his family and all who love him is incalculable but, whilst praying for his safety, Christians recognise the pattern of God's way. No more British people have been held hostage, but Terry Waite has paid the price and shown the costly path of Christian love – *agapé*.

> ### COURSEWORK
> 1. Find out all you can about Quakers, their beliefs and practices. Try to join them for worship one day. There is probably a Friends' Meeting House in your locality where you will be made welcome. Then write at length about what you have discovered.
> 2. Find out about the work of Amnesty International. You will find the address at the back of the book. Describe their work. You may be able to invite a speaker from a local group. Write at length about the work of the organisation and, *in consultation with your parents*, decide whether you yourself could help in their work.

Red Cross

Everyone is familiar with the badge of the Red Cross, but how much do you really know about the organisation? Our own British Red Cross Society, which was founded in 1870, is part of the much wider international Red Cross organisation.

This owes its origin to a Swiss banker, Jean Henri Dunant, who in 1862 published an account of the sufferings on the battlefield of Solferino in the Franco-Austrian war. It was entitled *Un Souvenir de Solferino* and urged the formation of a society of voluntary workers who would be available and trained to help the wounded in times of war.

The following year an international conference was held in Geneva attended by delegates from sixteen different nations at which a provisional programme was drawn up. A year later (1864) another conference was held, this time of diplomats, at which the Geneva Convention was drawn up and signed. It was agreed that in times of war the sick and wounded, whatever their nationality shold be cared for and that respect should be shown towards those looking after them, towards buildings sheltering them and transport conveying them to safety. Later these provisions were extended to war at sea and included the shipwrecked among those to be protected. Further revision was carried out in 1929 and again in 1949 when protection for civilians was also included.

This fourth convention has now been ratified by 140 countries. The sign of the red cross on a white background was adopted as a symbol of neutrality. The colours are those of the Swiss flag in reverse. In 1876 Turkey took up the idea but adopted a Red Crescent as its emblem, an idea which has spread to other Muslim countries. The organisation's motto is '*inter arma caritas*'.

The work of national bodies is co-ordinated by the International Red Cross Committee which meets every four years. It consists of twenty-five Swiss citizens and its meetings are attended by delegates from national societies and representatives of the governments of nations who have signed the Geneva Convention.

What kind of work does the Red Cross do?

In times of war they are active in dealing with enquiries about prisoners of war. Ask any older people known to you who were prisoners of war during World War Two what they know about the Red Cross and they are likely to remember food parcels which came to them in their camps. Civilians will remember letters received from friends in enemy-occupied territory via the Red Cross which brought news at a time when other forms of communication were out of the question. Hospital ships bringing wounded troops back from French harbours in 1940 were painted white with red cross symbols emblazoned on their funnels instead of being camouflaged in shades of grey like troop ships. It was expected that the symbol would be respected, though this did not always happen.

The Red Cross has many peace-time tasks as well. The Society is active in caring for disabled servicemen. They help with ambulance services, provide first aid at public gatherings of all kinds and help in work connected with hospitals. Some hospital libraries are run by the Red Cross. Most areas have a medical loans department run by them which provides equipment, such as bed pans, needed for short or long periods in home nursing. They organise blood donor sessions, provide meals on wheels, staff day centres, provide holidays for the disabled and are ready at all times to give help in the relief of disasters such as floods, hurricanes, major accidents. They provide training courses in first aid and in all these ways not only serve the community but also maintain their members in a state of preparedness for their primary task of helping the sick and wounded in times of war.

This World War II hospital carrier, HMHC Worthing *had, in peacetime, been part of the cross-channel passenger fleet sailing between Newhaven and Dieppe. She helped bring the wounded back from northern France in 1940. In our own times the royal yacht,* Britannia, *has been designed for easy conversion to a hospital carrier should the need arise.*

The United Nations Organisation

The United Nations Organisation is the most comprehensive peace-keeping body ever set up. Founded in 1945 immediately after the Second World War, it was based on an agreement between governments 'to save succeeding generations from the scourge of war'. A second purpose set out in the preamble to its Charter is 'to secure justice and advancement for all peoples'.

The constitution of the United Nations provides for a General Assembly of representatives of all member states which meets for three months every year, and a Security Council containing five permanent members and ten others elected for a term of two years. The founder members (China, France, Great Britain, the Soviet Union and the United States of America) have the right to veto decisions. These are serviced by a Secretariat headed by a Secretary-General (*find out the name and nationality of the present Secretary General*) elected by the General Assembly. All these are based in the United Nations building which stands on international territory in Manhattan.

The United Nations also has an International Court of Justice which sits in The Hague.

A number of agencies have been created by the United Nations to meet the needs of the world. Some of these are concerned with operations, such as communications, air safety regulations, meteorological research, which must be globally organised. Some, such as the office of the High Commissioner for Refugees, deal with distress caused by continuing difficulties and conflicts. The largest agencies work continually to fulfil the aim of bettering conditions for all people. Examples are the Food and Agriculture Organisation (FAO), the World Health Organisation (WHO), the UN Children's Emergency Fund (UNICEF) and the UN Educational, Scientific and Cultural Organisation (UNESCO). The most recently created agencies are the UN Environment Programme and the UN Centre for Human Settlements (Habitat). The agencies have their headquarters in different cities: Rome, Geneva, Paris, Vienna and the last two in Nairobi.

In 1948 the General Assembly adopted a Universal Declaration of Human Rights. This is a remarkable document and, if you decide to make a particular study of the United Nations you should certainly get hold of a copy (addresses at the back of the book). It sets out quite clearly the rights of *all* members of the human family – life, liberty, freedom from torture, equality before the law, including the right to be presumed innocent until proved guilty, the right to privacy and freedom of movement, the right to nationality, the right to marry and the right to consent to the choice of spouse, the right to own property, the right to freedom of thought, the right to work and the right to leisure, the right to education and many more. Article 30 states 'nothing in this Declaration may be interpreted as implying for any State, group or person any right to engage in any activity or to perform any act aimed at the destruction of any of the rights and freedoms set forth herein'.

Much of the work of the United Nations goes on quietly year in, year out and never makes the news. Many of you may have received or sent Christmas cards bearing the name UNICEF without really thinking much about what that organisation's work entails. Find out for yourselves. Inevitably any failures of the UN to keep the peace are blazoned across the headlines. Its successes deserve to be more widely-known.

The Third World

TO START YOU TALKING

Which of these statements reflect your own opinions?

1. People in the Third World are lazy and dishonest and could do more to help themselves.
2. Third World countries should trade to become prosperous.
3. The high birth rate in the Third World is responsible for their difficulties.
4. Improved education is the best form of Aid.
5. Drought is the main problem and we cannot change the weather.
6. If we send Aid to the Third World it is stolen before it reaches its destination.
7. Money sent to the Third World is wasted.
8. Charity begins at home and we've too many poor of our own to be able to help in the Third World.
9. The problem is too vast for individuals to be able to play any useful part.
10. I'd like to give a year or two of my life to service overseas before settling down to a career at home.

INFORMATION

1. THE BRANDT REPORT

In 1980 an important report was published called *North–South: A Programme for Survival.* Known by the name of the leader of the group of politicians who had met to consider the problem of world poverty, the Brandt Report describes a world divided into rich and poor. Broadly speaking Northern areas of the world are wealthy – Europe, the United States, Japan (but including also Australia and New Zealand), and southern countries (South America, Africa, Asia) are poor. The countries of the 'south' are known as the Third World or 'developing' countries. Three quarters of the world's population live in developing countries where the birth rate is high but life expectancy low. Where parents have to rely on their children to support them when they themselves can no longer work, they will have as many as possible since they know few will survive. In fact 15 million children under the age of 5 die each year of hunger. *Think about that figure. What is the population of the largest town you know well? How many towns of that size does 15 million represent? And that mortality figure includes only children under the age of five.* Life expectancy in the Third World is, on average, 50 years compared with 70+ in the northern hemisphere.

2. FOOD

In Europe one in five adults suffers from over-eating whilst one in nine of the world's population is severely under-nourished. The earth produces enough grain for everyone to have 3,000 calories per day yet 500 million people live in absolute poverty. Because the rich world enjoys eating meat one-third of the grain produced on earth is fed to cattle, and the livestock in the rich world eat more grain than all the people of the Third World put together. The Brandt Report tells us that one and a half per cent of one year's expenditure on arms would provide all the farming equipment needed for Third World countries to become self-sufficient in food production.

Mother will be back in 2 or 3 hours. She has just gone to get you a cup of water!

STOWELL

3. WATER

As well as having food problems, Third World countries face difficulties over water supplies. Twenty-five *million* people die annually from water-related diseases and 2.4 *billion* have no adequate sanitation. It is difficult for people living in developed countries to imagine what it must be like to be without clean water yet nearly 2 billion people in the world are in that situation even though it is not difficult technically to bring a supply of clean water to a community. For the cost of one British Aerospace fighter aircraft one and a half million people could be provided with a safe water supply.

> ## TEST YOURSELF ON FACTS
> 1. What is the Brandt Report?
> 2. Name three Third World countries.
> 3. How many children under the age of 5 die of hunger each year?
> 4. Name three kinds of health care which would help rural communities in the Third World.
> 5. What is meant by a 'primary commodity'?
> 6. What is a transnational company?

4. HEALTH CARE

Lack of food and clean water inevitably lead to poor health and in the least developed countries there is a lack of basic health provision. The money spent on one jet fighter could provide 40,000 village pharmacies. The money spent in half a day on arms could eradicate malaria. So many of the things we take for granted — immunisation, ante-natal care, child health programmes and education in basic hygiene — are lacking in the villages. When a whole village was wiped out because hunger led people to eat sun-baked dung, we need to question priorities.

5. TRADE

Prosperity grows through trade but many Third World countries suffer from having once been colonies. More profit can be made from manufactured goods than from raw materials so, in the past, European countries took the primary commodities (= raw materials before they have been processed) from their colonies and used them to benefit themselves through manufacturing. For example, cotton was taken from India, processed in Lancashire cotton mills and then sold, some of it back to India, as manufactured goods. This situation still exists. For example, tea leaves are shipped to Europe, packed into tea bags and sold, even back to the country of origin, at a profit. Coffee beans are imported in bulk, turned into instant coffee to be resold at a profit. If Third World countries could afford to develop their own manufacturing industries they could benefit from their own primary commodities, but the powerful manufacturing nations are unwilling to give up their own profits by allowing this to happen. So the kind of situation develops which occurred in Guinea Bissau, West Africa, a few years ago. Groundnuts are grown there because the climate is suitable. These are a valuable source of protein but, because the country needed the money, the harvest was sold as a 'cash crop' to Western Europe. So urgent was the need for cash that local sales were banned. Europeans then fed the groundnuts to cattle, which then produced too much milk, which was then turned into milk powder and sent back to Guinea Bissau in the form of Aid to the Third World. *Can you think of a better way of helping?*

CHECK YOUR UNDERSTANDING

1. Why is the birth rate high in Third World countries?

2. Why, if there is enough grain to feed everyone in the world, are people in the Third World starving?

3. Why is it important for Third World countries to have their own manufacturing industries?

4. What are the risks for a nation of being dependent on a single commodity?

---

6. TRANSNATIONAL COMPANIES

One-third of world production is in the hands of companies which span several nations. These companies control all levels of production and sale. Land is bought from local people and cash crops are grown. Third World countries are then obliged to sell their primary commodities at prices set by international companies which may well control *all* the trade in a particular product. In return they receive on average only 15 per cent of the final price of the product, the rest going to the transnational corporation. Some countries are dependant on a single commodity so a poor harvest or sharp drop in the world price of that commodity can have serious consequences. Zambia depends on copper for 96 per cent of its exports. Seventy per cent of Ghana's earnings come from cocoa. Sudan relies on cotton for 60 per cent of its trade. Growing sugar beet in industrialised countries can play havoc with the price of cane sugar. Releasing a bumper crop into the world market can ruin countries which rely on exporting cane sugar.

WHAT DO YOU THINK?

What would you reply to people who said:

(a) 'Contraception is the answer to problems of hunger.'

(b) 'Droughts and floods are the reason for poverty and we cannot do anything about those.'

(c) 'Send the food mountains to the Third World.'

(d) 'Problems of the Third World are none of my business.'

---

7. ACTION

So what, in practical terms, can individuals do?

(a) Support the work of relief organisations like Oxfam, Christian Aid, War on Want, CAFOD, etc. Volunteer to take a collecting tin as soon as you are old enough.

(b) Find out if somebody near you sells Traidcraft or Tear Fund goods and buy them. Some, like tea, coffee, sugar can be bought on a regular basis; others would make good presents.

(c) At election times ask parliamentary candidates about their parties' commitment to the Third World. Make them realise voters care about the issue. Write to your MP when issues such as Aid to the Third World are before parliament.

(d) Consider the possibility of working in the Third World youself. Get in touch with VSO for details.

(e) Give part of your earnings regularly, week by week, to a relief organisation. They will provide a box if you ask them.

(f) Keep yourself informed about Third World issues and be prepared to discuss them with other people.

CHRISTIAN PERSPECTIVES

SUGGESTIONS FOR BIBLE STUDY

Ex. 20.1–17   Matt. 25.31–46
Deut. 15.7–11   Luke 3.10–13; 10.25–37;
Amos 5.24; 7.7–8   12.16–21;16.19–31

1. OLD TESTAMENT

(a) Exodus 20

Which commandments deal with murder and stealing? Are they applicable to the way prosperous countries treat the Third World?

(b) Deut. 15.7–11

What provision for the poor is made in this passage?

(c) Amos 7.7–8

In the eighth century B.C. the rich in Israel ignored the great gulf which existed between them and the poor. The prophet Amos had a vision of a plumbline being held against a wall, i.e. a standard of uprightness by which the nation was to be measured. How would the behaviour of the rich countries towards the Third World stand up to the plumbline treatment?

2. NEW TESTAMENT

(a) Luke 10.25–37

Consider honestly which role in the story this country plays if the countries of the Third World are the victims. Are we the bandits responsible for their plight, people passing by on the other side, good Samaritans – or all three?

(b) Matt. 25.31–46

Mother Teresa often refers to this parable and her own work is rooted in her understanding of it.

(c) Re-read all the other passages listed from St Luke. They have all been used already in Unit 25. Now apply their teaching to the question of helping the Third World.

(d) Charity may begin at home but 'home' is this planet. Christians believe that as they know what is going on in the Third World they have no excuse for ignoring their brothers' need.

Now look at the questions at the beginning of this Unit again. Have your opinions changed now that you know more about the issues? Help to educate other people.

COURSEWORK

1. Find out about the work of one of the relief organisations helping in the Third World, e.g. CAFOD, Christian Aid, Oxfam, Save the Children Fund, War on Want (addresses at the back of this book. Enclose a stamp.)

Then write about it at length answering the following questions:
(a) When and why was the organisation founded?
(b) What kind of projects does it help?
(c) Are any conditions imposed before Aid is granted?
(d) How is aid distributed?
(e) What percentage of the Charity's income is used for administration?
(f) What are the Charity's sources of income?
(g) How can *you* help?

2. Find out about the life and work of Bob Geldof in relation to Aid for the Third World.

3. *Now is the time to use up the cuttings from magazines which you collected for the work in Unit 21.*

Make a wall chart using collage techniques. At the centre have two circles side by side. On one stick outlines of the countries of the 'North' and on the other countries of the 'South'. Use your collection of pictures to make a collage of the way of life in both parts of the world. In the centre, between the two worlds, hang a plumbline and take one of the quotations from Amos as a title.

Traidcraft

The first thing to strike you about this company should be the spelling of its name. *Be careful to continue spelling the word TRADE correctly!* The spelling TRAIDcraft tells you something about the function of the organisation which aims to help the Third World by encouraging fairer trading between countries of the 'north' and 'south'. It was started in 1979 by a group of people who were disturbed by the injustices existing in trade between rich and poor.

Remind yourselves of what has been said in Unit 32 about the poor prices paid for primary commodities compared with those paid for manufactured goods. The example used there was tea compared with tea bags. One of the countries from which Traidcraft buys tea is Mauritius. This tea has been packed in Mauritius and the packing process provides employment for the handicapped. So Mauritius benefits from its own primary commodity.

Help is also given where possible to coffee growers. It takes a lot of money to start a manufacturing or processing plant and if, for example, you buy Campaign Blend Instant Coffee from Traidcraft you are supporting an instant coffee plant in East Africa itself. Not only do the manufacturers benefit but the farmers also receive a fair price for their coffee beans. All too often coffee is grown on large estates where the pickers earn very little and live in great poverty but Traidcraft will only do business with people who do not exploit their workers. Traidcraft products are supplied by community enterprises, producer co-operatives and even small family groups. All must meet certain standards, i.e. they must:

1. Be organised for the benefit of their workers.
2. Pay wages which are good or above average for the locality.
3. Provide satisfactory working conditions.
4. Make products which have commercial potential.
5. Be concerned for the welfare of workers and their families.

Furthermore they must not be paying unreasonable fees to middle-men.

Sikas – used as planters or as a method of storage – made by Bangladesh village women, available from Traidcraft.

Many products sold by Traidcraft enable people in the Third World to earn money from using traditional skills. For example in Agra, home of the Taj Mahal, live the descendants of Persian craftsmen who were brought to India to create this beautiful building. These workers are skilled in stonework inlaid with mother of pearl and there is a steady demand for their beautiful stone vases, plates and souvenir boxes. Traidcraft imports these from Tara Projects, a local organisation which exports for a number of craft groups. Tara pay fair prices to the workers and also try to encourage community organisation.

In Bangladesh sikas made from locally grown jute are the normal method of storage in village homes. Through Traidcraft these traditional hand-made products reach a wider market and the local people benefit from having the value of their labour added to the value of the raw material.

Another programme specifically offering help to poor families in Bangladesh is the making of wheatstraw pictures. It is aimed at young unmarried girls who would otherwise have to marry at 13 or 14 to ease the economic burden on their families. Wheatstraw art consists of tiny pieces of wheat stuck into a delicate mosaic pattern. The straws of wheat are first shaved and flattened with a chisel. Golden, brown and black shades are made by burning the straw on a hot plate. Each piece is then cut and stuck individually onto card or stretched black cloth. A small card will take about 45 minutes to make. The girls work in small groups and may well earn more in a month than their fathers can. Through

providing an important addition to the family budget the pressure for early marriage is removed.

Traidcraft products are not cheap. In the 'rich' world to which we belong we have become accustomed to prices based on cheap raw materials and mass production. Is it right that the poor should subsidise the rich in this way?

One product sold by Traidcraft which is not imported from the Third World is paper. They buy it from recycling mills in Britain and West Germany. Seventy per cent of paper could be recycled but we go on cutting down trees instead, thus increasing the rate at which forests are disappearing. You will find more about the importance of trees in Unit 35. They are important in the Third World, not only as building material but also as fuel. Furthermore they protect the soil. So by NOT importing from the Third World we are helping them and also playing a part in conserving the world's natural resources.

Traidcraft is only one of many organisations concerned to make us aware of the gap between 'north' and 'south'. They work in conjunction with such organisations as Christian Aid and CAFOD to support manufacturing and exporting groups where there is a real commitment to personal and community development. They have many stories to tell of enterprises in the Third World. Why not investigate further for yourselves? There is a small charge for their catalogue but it is full of information about enterprises in the Third World as well as showing you an exciting range of things to buy. You will find addresses in the notes at the back of this book.

Mother Teresa

When Mother Teresa came to London she found people dying in the streets, and even in their own homes, unloved. 'Here you have a different kind of poverty,' she said, 'a poverty of spirit, of loneliness, and that is the worst disease in the world today, worse than tuberculosis or leprosy. We have to love.'

This extraordinary woman was born in 1910 in Skopje, Yugoslavia, of Albanian parents. At the age of 15, hearing about the work of Yugoslav Jesuits in Calcutta, she volunteered for the Bengal mission and at 18 became a novice in their convent in Darjeeling. She was sent to teach Geography in a school for high-caste Indian girls in Calcutta and eventually became principal. Gradually though she became aware of another vocation within her vocation to the religious life. She believed that God was calling her to serve him in the poorest of the poor.

She remembers 10 September 1946 as her 'Day of Decision'. It was then that she asked permission to be an unenclosed nun to work in the slums of Calcutta.

When permission was granted she went first to Patna for intensive nursing training, returning to Calcutta at the end of 1948. She was given permission to open her first slum school and the following year a Bengali girl joined her to form the nucleus of a new order, the Missionaries of Charity. These sisters in their white saris edged with blue stripes were soon to become a familiar sight not only in Calcutta but in slums throughout the world – Venezuela, Ceylon, Tanzania, Rome, Australia and – yes – in London too. Their work is done with an unforced joy and enthusiasm which are a perfect expression of Christian love – *agapé*.

Mother Teresa does not want people to focus on her own life. The work she does is Christ's work, serving him in the poorest of the poor and the circumstances of her own life are unimportant. Look again at the parable of the sheep and the goats (Matt. 25.31–46). It is often quoted by Mother Teresa and is the basis of her own understanding of her work. As she tends the dying, cares for lepers, rescues new-born babies from dustbins, she is serving Christ in the outcast. Her love for them is God's love, flowing through her.

She never worries about money; when needed it seems to arrive. Mother Teresa sees this as God providing for his own work. When the pope visited India he gave her the white limousine he had used in his travels. She raffled it and made enough money to start a leper colony. She has won many international awards for her work including the Nobel Peace Prize. All prize money goes into the work. She is perhaps best known for her care of the dying. This work started when she picked up a woman from the streets who was being eaten by rats and ants and the hospital refused to take her in. Places could only be spared for those with hope of recovery. Many were dying on the streets. So she asked the city authorities to provide her with a building where she could take such people. They offered her a disused Hindu temple which she gratefully accepted. Today it is perhaps the best-known Home for the dying in the world. Many thousands have been taken there to die in peace, surrounded by love. All must first have been turned away from hospitals. Mother Teresa has never lost her love of teaching. She started a school in the Calcutta slums.

They had no building so met in a compound belonging to a slum family. On the first day she had five pupils. Now the sisters have over 500. Children are taught to read and are given lessons in elementary hygiene – a far cry from teaching geography to middle class girls.

Work among lepers has also grown from the five who first came to the sisters in 1957 to the many thousands they care for today. If the disease is diagnosed early it can be cured in under two years. The sisters run a rehabilitation centre to help those who have been cured and offer loving care to those where the disease has gone beyond such help.

In the early days people were sometimes patronising about this woman who went off to serve the poor in the slums. What difference could such a tiny drop in the ocean make to the problems of world poverty? She herself points out that the ocean would be smaller without that drop. Today even the hard-bitten recognise her influence. For Christians caught up in the confusions of life in the twentieth century Mother Teresa stands out as a reassuring example of the truth of the gospel. They see what can be achieved when Christ is taken at his word and followed in simplicity.

TO START YOU TALKING

1. Take a wastepaper basket out into the school grounds at the end of the lunch hour and see how much litter you can collect in ten minutes.
2. Make a list of places defaced by graffiti.
3. Discuss the reasons why people spoil their environment in these ways and suggest ways of dealing with the problem.
4. Try to find out how much your own school has to spend in a year on restoring this kind of damage.

INFORMATION

Both litter and graffiti spoil the environment which is under constant threat from pollution of all kinds. The effects of pollution cross national boundaries. Welsh farmers found their sheep affected by the nuclear disaster at Chernobyl in the Soviet Union; Norwegian forests and lakes suffer from the effect of acid rain caused by sulphur oxides emitted from power stations in the United Kingdom; pollution of the Rhine in the industrial areas of Germany kills fish in Holland.

Here are some widespread examples of pollution to start you thinking about the issue.

1. ACID RAIN

The trees in Germany's Black Forest are dying because of acid rain and 18,000 lakes in Sweden now have no fish from the same cause. Britain is the worst offender in Western Europe in producing the sulphur oxides which eventually fall as acid rain. This rain damages the stonework of old buildings and releases aluminium into the soil which then finds its way into water supplies. This aluminium is poisonous.

Britain has not joined the Thirty per cent Club, a group of European countries committed to reducing emissions of harmful substances from power stations by 30 per cent. Instead, at a cost of £200 million the United Kingdom intends reducing sulphur emissions by about 14 per cent by the end of the century.

2. NUCLEAR DUMPING

The European Nuclear Energy Agency predicts that 160,000 tonnes of spent nuclear fuel will have built up by the year 2000. It is more radioactive than the original uranium and is likely to stay that way for about three *million* years. At the moment Britain is storing spent fuel at Sellafield.

Until 1983 *low*-level waste was dumped at sea. Even now 1.2 million gallons of slightly radioactive waste is pumped into the Irish Sea each day. The government is looking for suitable sites for burying low-level waste but, not surprisingly, local people rise up in wrath if there is rumour of a possible site on their doorsteps. Once sites have been established there will be inevitable danger in transporting nuclear waste from one place to another. Can you justify creating and handing on a problem of this magnitude to future generations?

TEST YOURSELF ON FACTS

1. Give two examples of pollution which cross national boundaries.
2. Give two examples of the effect of acid rain.
3. For how many years is nuclear waste likely to remain radioactive?

WHAT DO YOU THINK?
Do the possible dangers of nuclear power outweigh its benefits?

3. OIL

Seabirds and wildlife habitats around the coast are damaged when there is an oil spill. Birds find their feathers clogged with oil which destroys their natural waterproofing. They are then unable to swim or fly and starve to death. Using chemicals to disperse oil slicks may harm natural habitats more than leaving the oil where it is. In estuaries seaweed and algae are an important part of the food chain. Oil prevents their growth and so reduces the food for birds and fish. Many believe that patterns of evolution could be affected.

4. OZONE

In 1987 through the United Nations Enviroment Programme agreement was reached to limit the production of chlorofluorocarbons (CFCs). These have been used in refrigerator compressors, aerosols and air-conditioning equipment for years but when they are released into the atmosphere they destroy ozone molecules in the upper atmosphere. Ozone blocks some of the ultraviolet rays from the sun and thinning the layer increases the risk of skin cancer as well as causing damage to crops. Agreement has been reached to reduce the use of CFCs by 30 per cent while an alternative is sought.

5. WATER

Of 365 British beaches monitored, only 27 satisfied

CHECK YOUR UNDERSTANDING

1. Describe the threat to ozone and the danger of allowing the layer of it to become thin.
2. Write a paragraph about the pollution of water.
3. What are the dangers of oil slicks on the coast?
4. Write a paragraph to explain how Naboth's attitude to his land differed from Jezebel's.

EEC standards. The rest, including famous holiday resorts, are contaminated by sewage to an unacceptable level. Off the east coast British sewage is destroying the life of the sea and contaminating shell fish. The sewage is then washed onto the shores of the continent and, as other nations bordering the North Sea treat their sewage before discharging it, Britain is very unpopular with her neighbours. The government is to spend £250 million on dealing with this problem but the money is to be spent on lengthening outlet pipes rather than treating the sewage itself.

Inland, ten per cent of groundwater in Britain is no longer fit for human consumption as industrial waste and agricultural chemicals find their way into rivers.

CHRISTIAN PERSPECTIVES

SUGGESTIONS FOR BIBLE STUDY
Gen. 1 and 2   1 Kings 21.1–21
Ps. 24.1

1. RESPONSIBILITY

According to Gen. 1 and 2 what responsibilities are given to mankind by God?

2. PARTNERSHIP

To whom does the psalmist say the world belongs? Christians believe that people are *partners* in creation not lords of creation. In fact human beings are only one of some two million species who share our environment.

3. STEWARDSHIP

The Israelites were aware that they were stewards of the land, caring for it on God's behalf during their lives and handing it on to the next generation. In the story of Naboth's vineyard King Ahab, who should have known better, allowed himself to be over-ruled by Queen Jezebel. She came from Phoenicia, a commercial country and did not understand Naboth's attitude to the land of his vineyard. The prophet Elijah was sent to remind the king of his responsibility.

The need to balance commercial or purely selfish interests against the need to protect the environment is still a problem in contemporary life.

COURSEWORK

1. Choose one of the major enquiries going on at national level at the time when you are studying this Unit. Suitable issues which are likely to recur at regular intervals are, for example:

   (a) Those concerning the routing of major new roads (should the 'easier' route be chosen even though it goes through an area of outstanding natural beauty, as in the case of the Okehampton by-pass, or should a less convenient but less damaging route be taken?)
   (b) The extension of coalfields into Green Belt land (as has been proposed by the National Coal Board in Warwickshire) or the freeing of Green Belt land for housing developments.
   (c) The Channel Tunnel which will have to balance the need for a huge terminal with the attendant increase in traffic in an area of outstanding natural beauty, against the needs of local people and the environment.

   Having chosen your topic,

   (a) Make a file of newspaper cuttings and keep an eye on the correspondence columns of the serious newspapers.
   (b) Write to the conservation organisations for information about their involvement (addresses at the back of this book).
   (c) Follow up parliamentary reports and, where appropriate, write to your MP.
   (d) Make your own analysis, using as many facts as possible to help you draw your own conclusions. You should present two sides of the argument, i.e. commercial and conservation. Apply the relevant Christian perspectives to the case – you have plenty to choose from in this book and should go through it slowly and carefully, picking out whichever ones are relevant – and end with your own reasoned decision.

2. Take a local issue and find out all you can about the way in which people can make their views known and how decisions are reached.

   Choose a planning application in your neighbourhood which interests you and follow its progress. You can go and listen to the local council debating the issue and hear what factors carry most weight as they make their decision. Are they primarily the commercial ones or is there awareness that we have a responsibility for the future? Invite a local councillor to come to school to answer questions.

   Then present your views in as interesting a way as possible.

1. Should fox hunting be abolished?
2. Are experiments on animals for medical purposes justified?
3. Are circuses cruel?

INFORMATION

1. FACTORY FARMING

Domestication of wild animals, which has been going on for more than 4000 years, has now led to factory farming. You have to consider whether this can be justified morally.

Intensively reared animals receive controlled attention – lighting, temperature and ventilation are all monitored accurately, and adequate food must be given regularly to maintain production. It is therefore possible to argue that animals are better off under controlled conditions than fending for themselves in the wild. On the other hand, consider these facts:

(a) Battery hens

Chicken are gregarious and sociable by instinct. In a battery, four hens are kept in a cage only 40 cms wide with a wire floor, i.e. giving 10 cm width to each bird although the wing span of a chicken is 80 cms. They cannot perch or scratch or enjoy any of their natural behaviour. In order to increase laying, lights are kept on for 18 hours each day but frustration and boredom lead to cannibalism among the birds. Ninety per cent of commercial eggs are produced in this way. They are cheaper but do not compare in flavour with free range eggs. A viable alternative to batteries is the strawyard system which enables the birds to run about under controlled conditions but with enough freedom to enjoy natural behaviour. *Would you be prepared to pay more for eggs for the sake of hens being able to lead a more natural life? Does it matter?*

(b) Pigs

Pigs are intelligent creatures with a sense of fun. They enjoy running around and wallowing. When intensively reared, sows are kept in tie-stalls where they are held by an iron collar. They lie on a concrete floor, slatted at the back to allow dung to fall through and are allowed no exercise at all. When the time comes for the sow to give birth, she is put into a farrowing crate where there is even less room to move. Her piglets are removed when they are a fortnight old and are put in cages very similar to battery cages where they stay until it is time for them in turn to be fattened. As soon as possible the sow is served by the boar and the whole cycle starts again.

Find out about calves for yourselves. As yet sheep are not intensively reared.

All these practices are legal, although they may infringe codes of practice established in 1971. A Committee set up to investigate the treatment of farm animals issued a report (the *Brambell Report*) in 1965. It made many recommendations but most of them were ignored. When codes of practice are voluntary they do not have the force of law.

TEST YOURSELF ON FACTS
1. What is the wing span of a chicken?
2. How many hens may be kept in a battery cage 40 cms wide?
3. What is a strawyard?
4. What did the Brambell Committee investigate?

CHECK YOUR UNDERSTANDING
1. *What are the benefits for animals in factory farming?*
2. *Explain how factory farming thwarts the animals' natural instincts.*
3. *Find out the meaning of 'vivisection' and say whether you think it is justified.*

2. EXPERIMENTS ON ANIMALS

The issue of the use of animals in medical research poses many questions. For example many people are comparatively untroubled by the use of rats but become very heated if rabbits, cats or dogs are used in research. Is there really any difference? Under the Cruelty to Animals Act of 1876 research laboratories need a licence from the Home Secretary before they may carry out experiments on live animals. Three and a half million experiments of this kind are carried out every year, eighty per cent of them without anaesthetic.

In recent years public concern has been expressed at the use of animals in experiments needed for cosmetics. Rabbits have been used in testing the effect of shampoo ingredients. Irritant drops are inserted into the animals' eyes, which are clamped open, to assess the damage. Where do we draw the line? Human life can be saved because of research carried out on animals but how do we find a balance between the extent of the pain inflicted on the animal and the importance of the research? If results could be shared it would save duplication of experiments but this might mean sharing information with commercial competitors. People have to choose between commercial competition and compassion. Where do you stand?

CHRISTIAN PERSPECTIVES

SUGGESTIONS FOR BIBLE STUDY

Gen. 1.24–31	Isa. 40.11
Deut. 25.4	John 10.14
Ps. 23	

1. The Creation stories in the book of Genesis express the idea that humanity has been given authority over creation to care for it on behalf of God. Caring involves reverence for life and loss of that sense of reverence results in the brutalising of human beings.

2. Copy out Deut. 25.4. What attitude to animals does this passage show?

3. Throughout the Bible the shepherd is presented as an example of loving care. Look up the suggested references. What do they tell us about shepherds? Are these ideas applicable to the way in which we treat animals?

WHAT DO YOU THINK?

Do you think animals have feelings which should be respected?

COURSEWORK

1. Write to any cosmetics manufacturer you choose and ask about their policy on animal experiments. (Body Shop products and those from Beauty without Cruelty, Revlon and Avon, are produced without the use of animal experiments.) When you receive a reply, work out your own response to their policy and then write a magazine article on 'The Price of Beauty'.

2. Read the following poem and answer the questions.

Two Performing Elephants

He stands with his forefeet on the drum
and the other, the old one, the pallid hoary
                female
must creep her great bulk beneath the
                bridge of him.

On her knees, in utmost caution
all agog, and curling up her trunk
she edges through without upsetting him.
Triumph! the ancient, pig-tailed monster!

When her trick is to climb over him
with what shadow-like slow carefulness
she skims him, sensitive
as shadows from the ages gone and
                perished
in touching him, and planting her round
                feet.

While the wispy, modern children, half-
                afraid
watch silent. The looming of the hoary far-
                gone ages
is too much for them.

                (D. H. Lawrence)

1. What is the purpose of the performance? Does it succeed?
2. Is it a worthy use of the animals? Why?/ Why not?
3. How does the poet show where his own sympathies lie?
4. Express your own feelings about circuses in any way you find effective, e.g. painting, a poem of your own, or arrange a debate on 'Circuses should be abolished'.

Does it matter that year by year more and more species become extinct? For example, the rhinoceros and the elephant need protection if they are not to vanish forever. Nearer home, bats, cowslips, wild orchids and butterflies are all under threat. Think of reasons why we should bother to save them.

INFORMATION

1. NATURE UNDER THREAT

(a) Trees

The hurricane which struck southern England in October 1987 destroying over 15 million trees in one night opened people's eyes to the landscape they had lost. It was also a reminder of human powerlessness in the face of an element beyond human control. Even when fresh trees were planted people were aware that few if any of them would live to see the new trees grow as tall and lovely as those that had been destroyed. It was a brief and disturbing reminder that we are not on this earth for very long and that future generations can only receive what we pass on to them. It was not only trees and plants which suffered as a result of the hurricane. Trees provide the habitat for hundreds of other creatures. Oak trees for example support up to 300 species of invertebrates and so attract other wild life such as birds and squirrels. *Don't let your mind slip over that figure of 300. How many classes in your school does it represent? Imagine each person to represent a different species. That is the number of different species you might find in a single oak tree.* When a tree is destroyed all those creatures are at risk. Some far-sighted landowners left a few fallen trees to provide a habitat for those displaced species while young trees are growing; most wanted to tidy up and forget the destruction as quickly as possible, burning and so wasting timber which had taken centuries to grow.

(b) Hedgerows

We lose sight of a time scale beyond the human life span. Hedges are another inheritance which can be quickly lost. They provide a rich natural habitat, yet during the past forty-five years at least 150,000 kilometres of hedgerows (i.e. more than three and a half times round the world) have been removed. It is easier for farmers to operate in large fields and the hedgerows are not protected by law. But is the farmer's convenience all that matters? A landscape which has been passed on to us over many centuries can be changed beyond recognition by a single landowner and there is no control. Think of the birds' nests which are destroyed; of hedgerow flowers lost forever from the countryside; of the rabbit, fox and badger holes which used to be hidden in hedgerows. All are disturbed when a hedge is grubbed up, some beyond recovery.

Country dwellers are familiar with the sight of roads and lanes covered with topsoil washed off the fields where once hedgerows would have prevented such loss. Topsoil takes centuries to develop and become rich and fertile but now it is being lost because of our failure to understand the interdependence of Nature.

(c) Flowers

Our native flowers are also at risk. Primroses, cowslips, poppies were once a common sight in the countryside but now in some areas have become more rare as pasture, converted to arable use, is treated with herbicides.

(d) Birds

Similarly, if wetlands (such as the Somerset Levels) are drained to provide more arable land (which we have been doing at the rate of 100,000 hectares per annum) the natural habitat of water birds and waders is destroyed.

2. REASONS FOR CONSERVATION

There are at least three good reasons why nature conservation is essential:

(a) Farmers need to preserve the fertility of the soil. *Find out about areas of the world where intensive farming has produced a dust bowl.* Fertility depends on many factors, not least on micro-organisms in the soil itself, which can be carelessly destroyed.

(b) Many scientific discoveries of great benefit to humanity have been made by studying natural life.

CHECK YOUR UNDERSTANDING

1. *Explain the reason for leaving some fallen trees after the great hurricane.*
2. *Why are hedgerows important?*
3. *Why is converting pasture land to arable use a threat to wild flowers?*
4. *Think of three important scientific discoveries which have been made by studying natural life.*

It would be arrogant to assume we have nothing more to learn from Nature so that we need no longer bother to care for living things.

(c) The sheer enjoyment of beauty. Walking, climbing, camping, sailing, fishing, birdwatching are all popular pursuits. They help us to relax and restore a sense of proportion in a madly rushing world. A sense of wonder is a first and important step in coming to know God.

For all these reasons **conservation** (= preserving from damage or loss) is high on the agenda in the modern world.

3. THE LAW

The law in recent years has tried to hold a balance between the needs of the natural world and the needs of people. For example:

1954 Protection of Birds Acts protect all birds, their

nests and their eggs. The only exceptions are game birds in the shooting season and any birds which are widely regarded as pests.

1975 Conservation of Wild Creatures and Wild Plants Act makes it illegal to dig up wild plants without authority. Certain endangered species of animals, such as the otter, are also covered by the Act. By the end of 1986 a Nature Conservancy Council report identified a further 32 species, including dormice, whales, dolphins, adders, wild cats, which need stronger legal protection.

1981 Wild Life and Countryside Act provides for farmers to receive compensation if they are prevented from making full use of their land because of conservation requirements. Most farmers do their best to help conservation efforts but without some such encouragement there is inevitably temptation to turn a blind eye to, for example, the rare wild orchids beginning to bloom in a field needed for agricultural purposes.

4. APPRECIATION

Don't just sit glued even to splendid Nature films on television. Go out and *notice* the natural world. Use all your senses. Look closely at, for example, a single flower, leaf, insect, spider's web and make yourself aware of the perfection of its form and colour. Be aware of texture — the bark of trees, the differing textures of the coats of cats, dogs, horses. Use your nose to help you appreciate the world around you — pleasant and unpleasant. Turning to hearing, how many bird songs can you recognise? Get hold of a record of birdsong and improve your knowledge. Do you even notice

---

COURSEWORK

Once you have become aware of the joy of natural beauty for yourself you will want to protect it. Then is the time to act. Find out about the many different organisations concerned with conservation. Addresses are provided at the end of the book but first ask about your own county's Trust for Nature. The address will be available at your public library, though it is very probable that your school is already affiliated to it. If not, perhaps you yourselves could form a pressure group to bring this about. Find out what is going on and join in. You may be able to undertake a study of a particular problem in the light of the requirements of your syllabus. You would need to ask yourselves:

(a) How has the problem in question arisen?
(b) Give an account of the facts of the case.
(c) What are the points of view of any opposing factions?
(d) What moral justification is there on each side?
(e) What light do the Christian perspectives you have studied in this book throw on the issues involved?
(f) Make up your own minds as to what should be done and give reasons for your decision.

TEST YOURSELF ON FACTS
True or False?
1. All birds without exception are protected by the 1954 Protection of Birds Acts.
2. It is legal to shoot birds which are pests.
3. It is illegal to dig up any wild plant.
4. Otters are a protected species.
5. Farmers suffer financially if they support conservation.

birds singing? Marvel at the volume of sound produced from such tiny bodies. And make yourself consciously aware of taste — apples, oranges, melons, peas newly scooped from the pod, and don't allow yourself to take such pleasure for granted.

WHAT DO YOU THINK?
What difference does it make if we are grateful?

CHRISTIAN PERSPECTIVES

Inevitably some of the finest expressions of human wonder at the beauty of Creation come from poets. Try reading some of the book of Job for yourself starting at chapter 38. William Blake is another poet who captures perfectly a sense of wonder at the natural world in the lines,

'To see a World in a grain of sand,
And a Heaven in a wild flower,
Hold Infinity in the palm of your hand,
And Eternity in an hour.'

(Auguries of Innocence)

Robert Browning goes a step further in seeking *purpose* in the beauty around him:

'You've seen the world
— the beauty and the wonder and the power,
the shapes of things, their colour, lights and shades
Changes, surprises, — and God made it all!
For what? Do you feel thankful, aye or no,
For the fair town's face, yonder river's line,
The mountain round it and the sky above,
Much more the figures of man, woman, child,
These are the frame to? What's it all about?
To be passed over, despised? or dwelt upon,
Wondered at? . . . This world's no blot for us,
Nor blank — it means intensely and means good:
To find its meaning is my meat and drink.'

(Fra Lippo Lippi)

Let the last word be with St Paul:

'Finally, brethren, whatsoever things are true, whatsoever things are honest, whatsoever things are just, whatsoever things are pure, whatsoever things are lovely, whatsoever things are of good report; if there be any virtue, and if there be any praise, think on these things.' (Phil. 4. 8. A.V.)

BIBLE REFERENCES *which appear in the text*

Genesis
1.1–2.4 pp.4,90
1.26-28 pp.9,13
1.24-31 p.92
2.2-3 p.62
2.4–3.21 p.34
2.15 p.59
2.18 pp.9,15
3 p.4
3.17-19 p.59
4.1-9 p.34
4.9 pp.13.62
9.5-6 p.71

Exodus
15.3 p.78
20.1-17 pp.6,68,85
20.8-11 p.62
20.12 pp.18,27
20.13 p.80
21.24 p.71

Leviticus
19.33-34 p.53

Deuteronomy
15.7-11 pp.57,85
25.4 p.92

Ruth p.53

1 Kings
21.1-21 p.90

Job
38 *et. seq.* pp.39,95

Psalms
23 p.92
24.1 pp.78,90
104.15 p.41

Proverbs
6.6-11 p.59
23.29-32 p.41

Isaiah
40.11 p.92

Jeremiah
38 p.80

Amos
5.7 and 10-12 p.57
5.24 p.85
7.7-8 p.85

Matthew
5.7 p.71
5.9 p.76
5.21-48 pp.6,27
5.27-30 p.9
5.31-32 p.29
5.38-42 pp.76,78
6.9 p.43
6.19-24 p.66
7.12 pp.32,44
18.21-35 p.71
19.1-12 p.29
20.1-16 pp.59,64
22.21 p.73
25.31-46 pp.36,41,53,57,73,85
26.51-52 p.80

Mark
3.31-35 pp.18,43
6.31 p.62
9.36-37 p.13
10.2-9 p.15
10.17-27 p.66
12.29-31 p.68
12.41-44 p.66

Luke
3.10-13 pp.66,85
10.7 p.64
10.25-37 pp.43,57,76,85
12.6-7 p.34
12.16-21 pp.66,85
15.11-32 pp.6,18,27,71
16.19-31 pp.64,66,85
23.43 p.36

John
2.1-12 p.15
9 p.39
10.14 p.92
11.25-26 p.36
13.1-17 p.60
14.1-3 p.36

Acts
2.44-46 p.23
4.32-35 p.23
5.29 p.73

Romans
12.6-8 p.23
12.17-21 p.78
13.1-5 pp.64,68,71
13.8-10 p.6
13.13-14 p.41
13 pp.71,73
14 p.49

1 Corinthians
6.19-20 p.9
7.10-11 p.29
11.11-12 p.47
12.4-11 p.23
13 p.9
15.12-17 p.36

2 Corinthians
8 and 9 p.66

Galatians
3.26-28 p.53
5.22 p.43
6.2 p.57

Ephesians
4.25-32 p.27
4.26-27 p.64
5.22-30 p.47
5.33–6.4 pp.18,27

Philippians
4.8-9 p.95

2 Thessalonians
3.6-12 p.59

1 Timothy
5.1 p.32
6.10 p.66

James
2.1-6 p.45

1 Peter
2.13-15 p.64

INDEX